WHAT OTHERS ARE S

Dr. James "Tahli Jusdu[1]"
University of Nebraska at Kearney:
"During many philosophical discussions with Al Herrin, I gained a new appreciation of traditional Native American worship. To me, my personal, Christian God and the God of the ancient Cherokees are one and the same.

Dr. Herrin writes with clarity and authority, and his book is a pleasure to read. It is my sincere belief that all who read this book will develop a deeper understanding of the Cherokee Way and will, without a doubt, experience a lasting impact on their spiritual lives."

Dr. Polly "Daksi[2]" Walker, Ph.D. in Peace and Conflict Studies - University of Queensland in Australia:
"Tsquayi (Dr. Al Herrin) speaks of this time, when our Cherokee Ancestors call upon us to practice deep, respectful communication with all. Before European colonization, our Cherokee people were strong in honoring the Spirits, other humans, and the natural world. This way of life has been suppressed, but it is not lost. The Ancient knowing remains and we can learn to participate in it. In this story of his journey, Tsquayi maps the way of the Spirit Path."

Adunto Tawodi[3], Cherokee Elder:
"Chief Tsquayi's words have strength, courage, power and the simplicity of the Truth. In my heart, I know that the spirits of the early ones are speaking to him".

---

[1] Tah-lee Jee-sdoo; Two Rabbits.
[2] Dahk-see; Box Turtle.
[3] Ah-dun-toe Tah-woe-dee; Spirit Hawk

CHEROKEE CALLING

A GUIDE FOR SPIRITUAL GROWTH

AL HERRIN

FIRST EDITION

 White Bear Publishing, Tahlequah, Oklahoma

CHEROKEE CALLING
A Guide for Spiritual Growth

By Al Herrin

Published by:

White Bear Publishing
Dept. B
17899 S 543 Rd
Tahlequah OK 74464 USA

Printed in the United States of America

Publisher's Cataloging in Publication Data
Herrin, Alan R.
        Cherokee Calling
        A Guide for Spiritual Growth
1. Cherokee Indians—Folklore
2. Religion and Mythology---American Indians
I. Title
398.2
HER

E99.C5H4   2004   2003-110028
ISBN 0-9623601-7-1 Soft cover

ABOUT THE AUTHOR

Dr. Al Herrin is a recognized authority on Cherokee arts, culture and religion, is a "National Living Treasure" of the Western Cherokee Nation, and is Peace Chief and Spiritual Advisor to the Cherokee Nation of Mexico. Al's wife, Frankie, is a direct descendent of the famous Cherokee Chief, John Ross and is a recognized authority on Cherokee history. Their home is near Tahlequah, Oklahoma, the Capitol of the Western Cherokee Nation.

Al has devoted much of his adult life to preserving the Cherokee culture. He learned to make traditional bows and arrows as a boy from Cherokee Elders. In the 1980's, Al was part of the Cherokee "Lost Arts" Project. As part of his work on that project, Al wrote the book, **Cherokee Bows and Arrows**, which helped restore the making and use of traditional bows and arrows to the Cherokee Nation, and to non-Cherokees throughout the United States and in many foreign countries. For his work, Al was designated a "Cherokee National Living Treasure" and "Master Craftsman" in Bows and Arrows by the Cherokee Nation in 1991.

In 2000, Al assisted Dr. Charles Rogers of Brownsville, Texas in his efforts to locate the lost tomb of Sequoyah which was found near the town of Zaragoza in Mexico. In 2001, Al and Frankie took part in the founding of the Cherokee Nation of Mexico with recognition from the Governments of Mexico and the State of Coahuila. Dr. Rogers was designated Principal Chief and Al was asked to serve as Peace Chief and Spiritual Advisor to the new Cherokee Nation of Mexico.

Al and Frankie continue their work of promoting identity and pride among the Cherokees and making non-Cherokees aware of Cherokee history, culture and achievements. This book is another part of those efforts.

ACKNOWLEDGEMENTS

First and foremost, I acknowledge the great debt I owe to my Cherokee people, Elders and others, who taught me the Cherokee Way. I have space to name only a special few of the many. They are Kawaya, Alex England, Richard McLemore, William Cabbagehead Sr., William Cabbagehead Jr., William Mose, Tommy Mose, Malinda Keys, Joanna Parris, Hastings Shade, Durbin Feeling, Jerry Day and my father, Raymon Herrin.

I acknowledge those who have subscribed to my White Bear Newsletter over the past thirteen years. Your financial and spiritual support allowed me to write this book.

Several people helped with the preparation of this book. I acknowledge the help of my wife, Frankie, for her many hours of proofreading, and for her spiritual insight and support. I acknowledge the help of my Brother Friend, Dr. Jim Miller for his insightful proofreading. I acknowledge the talent and insight of my friend, David Wren, for the art work in this book.

I dedicate this book to the Cherokee Elders and the Cherokee Spirits. Both will show us the way, if we will listen.

Al Herrin, Ph.D.
Tahlequah, Oklahoma
January, 2004

Cover and Illustrations by David Wren

TABLE OF CONTENTS

CHAPTER 1
THE CALLING

I, Al Herrin, also known by my Cherokee name of Tsquayi (Tsquah-yee; White Heron), have been called as a messenger to the Cherokees. This book is about that calling and those messages.

I was first aware of the calling as a young boy growing up in the Cherokee Nation in Oklahoma. I was shown a Spirit Path which I chose to follow through my life. Along my Spirit Path, I have been given messages for the Cherokee people. Those messages are guides for spiritual growth and peace: peace for humankind through reconciliation, and peace for each man and woman through greater understanding and sense of identity.

As the first step toward establishing that understanding and identity, I will define what I mean by "Cherokee". I believe that being Cherokee is much more than amount of Cherokee blood or being able to trace ones ancestry to the Dawes Commission Roll or some other document of enrollment. It is also more than skin color, facial bone structure or any other

9

physical characteristic. Cherokees are a mixture of people from different racial and ethnic backgrounds and, therefore, there is considerable variation in physical appearance. Cherokees being of mixed blood is not a recent phenomenon, but a tradition since ancient times. The ancient Anikilohi (Ah-nee-kee-loe-hee; Long Hair or Stranger) Clan of the Cherokees was made up largely of mixed-blood people.

The most important characteristics that define a person as Cherokee are mental and spiritual; what is in a person's mind and heart. A true Cherokee seeks an understanding of Cherokee culture and heritage, and believes there is truth, goodness and beauty in the Cherokee Way. The ancient Cherokees sought the Spirit Path, the way to becoming Aniyvwiya (Ah-nee-yuh-wee-yah; Real People, Human Beings). They were the children of the Spirits. They were a great nation, living in health, freedom and happiness. They lived in balance with Nature, the Spirit World[4], and one another.

I was born in 1936 and reared in the Cherokee Nation in Oklahoma. That was during the time when it was still considered a bad thing to be Cherokee. The stated policy of the U.S. Government, for generations, had been to force the acculturation of the Cherokees into the dominant American culture. A key part of that policy was to erase the traditional Cherokee culture. That policy was very effective and reached into most Cherokee homes. Many Cherokee parents became convinced that their children would be at a disadvantage in the white world if they spoke Cherokee or followed the traditional ways. Most of the Cherokee children I grew up with were deprived of their Cherokee culture and language, as had been

---

[4] The Spirit World is the spiritual counterpart of the physical universe.

their parents and grandparents before them. Today, fewer than five percent of Cherokees can speak the Cherokee language.

But, I was different. From an early age, I felt a calling toward things Cherokee. I sought out Cherokee speakers in order to learn as much of our language as I could. I sought out Elders who were willing to tell me the stories of the old days, and teach me the skills of hunting, fishing, and gathering wild plants for food and medicine. I learned how to make and shoot the traditional Cherokee bows and arrows. Most importantly, I learned about the Cherokee Spirit World. I learned to listen to the spirits and the spirits taught me and showed me my Spirit Path.

When I was thirteen years old, I had a vision of Yona Unega (Yoe-nah Oo-nay-gah; White Bear) who became my guide to my Cherokee Spirit Path. I have followed that path throughout my life. It has been a path of beauty, enlightenment, fulfillment and peace. I lived a life filled with amazing coincidences which, I believe, were not coincidences but the spirits acting in my life.

I spent most of my adult life as a teacher and writer, telling others about the wonders of Nature, the spirits and the Cherokee Way. A few years ago, I reached the age of retirement. I believed that, if I should die that day, I had no regrets. There was nothing that I would have done differently. I was content to rest.

But, the spirits had other things for me to do. In the autumn of 2000, I received a call from Dr. Charles "Jatlohi[5]" Rogers and thus began a remarkable journey, during which I assisted him in the discovery of the lost tomb of Sequoyah and the establishment of the Cherokee Nation of Mexico. Dr. Rogers was called to be their Principal Chief and I

---

[5] Jah-tloe-hee; Kingfisher.

11

was asked by Dr. Rogers and the Mexican Cherokees to serve as their "White" or "Peace" Chief and Spiritual Advisor.

In September of 2001, one of my oldest and dearest friends and mentors, Jerry Day, died in a tragic accident. Jerry was 84 years old and the last of the old bow-makers who taught me. Throughout his life, Jerry had dreams in which the spirits gave him messages. He told me about many of them over the years, and I never had reason to doubt their truth. On his last visit to our home, a few days before his death, Jerry told my wife, Frankie, and me that he was told, in a dream, that I was a "Chosen One"; chosen by the spirits to bring messages to the Cherokees.

I am humbled and grateful to play a small role in what, I believe, is a spiritual calling of the Cherokees. I hope that these messages will bring a new awareness of what it means to be a Cherokee, and a greater sense of identity and pride. I also hope that these messages can help to reconcile the spiritual beliefs of diverse peoples around the world, and help to bring peace to our world.

CHAPTER 2
THE SEARCH FOR IDENTITY

Today, the Cherokee people are the children of tragedy. We were once a great nation, living in health, freedom and happiness. We lived in balance with Nature, the Spirit World, and one another, but, the Aniyonega (Ah-nee-yoe-nay-gah; White People) came and took it all away.

They killed many of our people and drove us from our homes. They took the land, they cut the forests, they killed the wild animals, they polluted the waters and the air, and they even polluted the blood that flows through our bodies with their diseases.

Even worse than all those things, is that the Aniyonega took away the spirits that made us Cherokees. They said that we were savages and they had to "save" us, so they took away the ways of our ancestors. Instead of saving us, they destroyed us. They preached love and trust but practiced malice and deceit. They took our land and "gave" us other land and then they took that also. They took away our homeland and our freedom and put us in a prison they called "Indian Territory". They sent our children away to boarding schools so that they could not learn from the Elders and forbade them to speak our language. They "relocated" families from the Cherokee Nation to far away cities so they would forget how to be Cherokee. They tried to take away our Cherokee identity and recreate us in their own image.

The result of that brutal conquest and long term effort to erase the Cherokee culture has been the loss of identity by many Cherokees. Our roots in the past make us who we are, and our roots were taken away. If we do not know who we are and take pride in our heritage, then we are surely lost.

13

Many members of the Cherokee Nation, as well as many from other tribes of Native Americans, exhibit the symptoms of people who are lost and living lives that are out of balance. Alcoholism, drug abuse, poor self esteem and underachievement, school dropouts, teen pregnancy, child abuse, spousal abuse, depression, suicide, obesity, a wide range of health problems, poverty, and almost any other undesirable condition imaginable are rampant among Native American populations.

My goal, for much of my adult life, has been to help restore a sense of identity to the Cherokee people. To restore our identity, we need to restore our traditional arts, crafts, skills and language. My book **Cherokee Bows and Arrows** and my **White Bear Newsletter** were written to help fill those needs. I believe an equally important need is to restore our Cherokee spirits. That is one of my purposes in this book.

Belief in the Cherokee spirits does not imply the rejection of Christianity or other religions. Christianity has been part of the heritage and identity of many Cherokees for generations and will doubtless continue to be a part of Cherokee life. For example, my wife, Frankie, is an Elder in the Park Hill Presbyterian Church and I attend that church regularly. But, Christianity alone has obviously failed to provide all that is needed to bring identity and balance to many Cherokees. Our spiritual life must do more than prepare us for the time after death; it must help us to have mental and physical health, happiness and balanced, productive lives here on earth.

Whether we worship the Creator by the name of God, Allah, Yahweh, Great Spirit or some other name, we worship the same being. Let us be tolerant of the beliefs of others, live together in peace, and let God be the judge of who is right or wrong.

14

CHAPTER 3
SPIRIT PATH

The pre-Columbian Cherokees placed great value on the development of moral human values in all tribal members. They referred to themselves as Aniyvwiya (Ah-nee-yuh-wee-yah); "The Real People" or "Human Beings". A person's status in the tribe was not determined by birth, but by his or her development of virtue and the deeds which resulted. Many sought a Spirit Path which would guide their way to becoming Human Beings.

The characteristics of a Yvwi (Yuh-wee: Human Being) among the ancient Cherokees would be very similar to what we would consider a moral or good person today. I have listed thirteen characteristics of a Yvwi. There are probably other values that could be listed and probably no person succeeds in achieving perfection in all of the values I have listed, but, the list will serve to define what I mean by "Yvwi." The Yvwi is truthful, honest, reverent, respectful, loyal, brave, compassionate, generous, industrious, insightful, optimistic, clean and balanced.

The Spirit Path was the way for Cherokees to become Human Beings. As I have traveled my own Spirit Path, I have learned these things:

If you choose to follow a Spirit Path, it must be yours alone. If you search for it, it will be revealed to you.

You might think that your own Path will lead you away from others as they seek their Paths. But the Spirit Paths are not divergent; they are parallel. You will be constantly surprised at how your own thoughts and actions parallel the thoughts and actions

15

of others who are separated from you by distance and time. You will be reading a book written by someone years ago in a place far away and recognize the thoughts you had yesterday. You will receive a letter from someone far away that you have never met that has just discovered something you also have discovered. It is as if you are connected into a great network, and share the thoughts of others who are also moving toward becoming Human Beings.

You will discover that the boundaries of time, space, nationality, race, religious sect, sex, age, etc., will become less significant. Human Beings can be found within all groupings. You will become more akin to the Human Beings within each of those groups than you are to most of the people who are around you every day.

The instruction that you need to help you along your Path are imbedded in the daily information or stimuli you receive from everything you do or experience at home, work, school, church, play, vacation, etc. You need not worry that you will miss or not remember something that you need to help you along your Path; your mind will automatically select those things you need from your daily experiences and will assimilate those things into your personality. Every single thing that you need will be revealed to you without fail. Listen to the opinions, advice or teaching of others around you, but always trust your own intuition above all. It will determine, without fail, the value of any ideas or information to you.

You will never reach the end of your Spirit Path. But as you travel your Path, you will enjoy a life filled with satisfaction. You will receive the power and wisdom you need to accomplish things that nobody, including yourself, would have thought possible.

CHAPTER 4
PATH OF THE WHITE BEAR

The White Bear (Unega Yona; Oo-nay-gah Yoe-nah) first appeared to me in a dream when I was a boy of thirteen. The great bear reared to its hind legs before me and I drew my bow and prepared to drive my arrow up into its heart. Then, the bear spoke to me. It said, "Do not kill me. I will protect you." I lowered my bow and listened for the bear to speak again, but It did not speak again in words. Instead, it sent its words into my mind. It showed me a Spirit Path I could follow if I wished to become Yvwi (Yuh-wee; Human Being, True Person). That is a high goal for a Cherokee, or, I believe, for any person. The White Bear became my Spirit Animal and, since that time, it has guided me along that path and has protected me.

There have been signs that have guided me as I have traveled along my Spirit Path. Sometimes the signs came from persons, events, birds or mammals, sometimes from music, a painting, a photograph, or a scene I beheld, and sometimes from written words of poetry or prose. Somehow, I knew which of those, from among the many things I experienced each day, were signs, although, I often did not understand the significance of the sign until later. When I was a young man, the signs came infrequently. Now they come every day.

Fifty years after the White Bear first entered my life, the Great White Heron entered my life. During the month of May, 1998, the Great White Heron

(Tsquayi; Tsquah-yee) appeared to me several times. Where I live, in the Cherokee Nation of Oklahoma, I usually see a few Great White Herons each year, but they are not as abundant as the Great Blue Herons. One morning, as I took my walk at dawn, I saw thirteen Great White Herons and thirteen Great Blue Herons standing in the fog around a spring-fed pond.

The beauty and significance of the scene struck awe into me and I stood for several moments unable to move. The number thirteen has been of great significance to me throughout my life, and thirteen was a sacred number to the ancient Cherokees. In the many years I have walked near the pond, I had never before seen a Great White Heron on it and never more than two Great Blue Herons. In the following days, my wife, Frankie, and I saw many Great White Herons on the river near our house. Those were signs that the Great White Heron was to become a major factor, a Spirit Bird, in my life.

I have yet to determine the total significance of the Great White Heron in my life. But, I believe that it has been sent as a guide to me in my maturity, as the White Bear was sent to me in my youth. However, the entrance of the Great White Heron into my life has not diminished the power of the White Bear. It continues to guide my path, as the following incident demonstrates.

In June of 1998, my wife, Frankie, and I made one of our many trips to Alaska to visit our daughter Jane, her husband Todd and our two grandsons, Jake and Luke who lived near Homer, Alaska. None of us had been to Denali National Park, so, we drove from Homer up to the park.

The number of cars allowed inside the park is limited, so we took a bus tour. Denali, the mountain, was obscured by clouds, so we did not get to see it but the rest of the park, and particularly the wildlife, which paid no attention to our bus, was spectacular.

Halfway through the tour, we had seen hundreds of caribou and sheep, a few moose, some marmots, some ptarmigan, golden eagles, kestrels, ravens and probably some other creatures I don't recall, but we had seen no bears and everyone on the bus wanted to see bears.

I jokingly told Frankie I would use an old Cherokee bear call and I started chanting softly, "Yona, hadlvnihi? (Yoe-nah, hah-dluh-nee-hee; Bear, where are you?)." I had been doing this for only a few minutes when I spied two grizzly bears on the mountain above us and in the direction the road was heading! I pointed them out to our fellow passengers and the driver stopped the bus at the nearest point to them. To everyone's surprise, they came toward us and someone said, "They're white!"

They were indeed very light colored, almost white.

The park guide, who was also our bus driver, cautioned us to remain quiet because they didn't want the bears to become accustomed to human voices. The only sounds were the click of cameras and the whir of camcorders as the bears, a sow with a yearling cub, crossed the road within ten yards of the front of the bus and then began to eat fiddlehead ferns growing on the side of the road. They grazed back until they were even with my seat on the bus where I stood looking through the open window. The sow raised up and looked directly at me from less than ten feet away! Our eyes met for a moment and then, as if she had completed her mission, she and her cub ambled over the hill and we continued on our way.

After a few moments of silence, Frankie asked me, "Did She speak to you?" and I answered, "Yes, She introduced my brother to me."

CHAPTER 5
KAWAYA

I was a boy when I first saw Kawaya (Kah-wah-yah). I would sometimes ride my horse to the country store that was a few miles from our farm in the Cherokee Nation of Oklahoma and watch and listen to the old men playing checkers in the feed room behind the store. From two to six of them would usually be there, sitting on sacks of feed, smoking or chewing tobacco, playing checkers and talking in the Cherokee language. One day, a much older man with a deeply furrowed face was there watching. Later, I asked someone his name and was told he was called Kawaya, which translates in English, to Huckleberries.

Kawaya's name intrigued me because all the Cherokees I knew had a first and last name. Long ago, Cherokees usually had only one name but when the white men rounded up the Cherokees and made a tribal roll before removing them to Oklahoma, they made those Cherokees who had only one name take a first and last name before any provisions were issued.   Most Cherokees chose to change their names rather than let their families starve.

One day at the store, I was watching a checker game while Kawaya sat nearby, and he noticed the warts on my hands. I had several warts on my knuckles and fingers. They often got hit as I worked or played, so that one or more of them were bloody most of the time. Kawaya asked me if I would like to have him take away the warts. I asked him if it would hurt and he assured me it would not, so, I told him to go ahead.

With his finger, he fished some grains of corn out of the top of a burlap sack of shelled corn and proceeded to rub one of the warts with a grain of corn. Then he rubbed another wart with another grain of corn, and so on, until he had treated all the warts. I think he used two or three grains on some of the larger warts. He said nothing during the entire time, and when he had finished, he put the grains of corn in his pocket and resumed watching the checker game.

I asked him if that was all and he said yes. I waited and looked at the warts for a few minutes and finally asked him when the warts would go away. He smiled, as did the other old men, and said, that one day soon, I would notice that the warts were gone.

I decided that the whole thing was probably a joke the old men had cooked up to tease me so I quickly forgot about it. A few days later, I know it was not more than a week, I was in the barn starting to milk the cow when I suddenly noticed that the warts were gone! Furthermore, in the more than fifty years that have passed since that day, I have never had another wart on my hands.

Over the years that followed, I was attracted to the study of science in school and eventually received Bachelors, Masters and Ph.D. Degrees in Chemistry, Biology and the Behavioral Sciences. I worked and conducted research as a professional scientist and taught the sciences for many years. Yet, I still know of no scientific explanation for how Kawaya removed the warts from my hands.

The experience with the warts was the first of many experiences I would share with Kawaya. He became my mentor in my search for my Spirit Path.

CHAPTER 6
THE MESSENGERS

The following is a song of a Cherokee Shaman
of the Bird Clan, asking the Jisgwa (Jee-sgwah; Birds)
to bring messages from the Spirit World.

Come
Jisgwa,
Kin of mine;
Messengers from God.
Teach me how to read your message
And I will teach it to all who have ears to listen.

Come
White Dove,
Bird of Peace;
Messenger from God.
Sit upon my shoulder and speak:
Teach that all living things are our brothers and sisters.

Come
Raven,
Wise Old Bird;
Messenger from God.
Speak to me of ancient wisdom:
Honor to those who walked the Spirit Path before me.

Come
Nighthawk,
Dream Flyer;
Messenger from God.
Look for me into the future:
Teach me to read the signs that tell what the future holds.

Come
Eagle,
Wind Rider;
Messenger from God.
Teach me to walk the path of truth;
God and Nature are friends of the honorable man.

Come
Heron,
Chieftain Bird;
Messenger from God.
Show me the way to true balance;
Teach me cleanliness of my body and my spirit.

Come
Healers,
Butterflies;
Messengers from God.
Help me to find good medicine:
Let it heal the bodies and spirits of The People.[6]

---

[6] There are several hidden relationships to Nature in this song that would be expected to be good "medicine". After you read the following chapter on Numbers, come back and see if you can find them.

CHAPTER 7
NUMBERS

Scientists use mathematics, the manipulation of numbers, to understand the Natural universe. But, long before the advent of science, mankind was fascinated by numbers and believed that certain numbers are mysteriously related to Nature, the Spirit World and their lives and thus be good or bad "luck" or "medicine".

The number seven is probably the best known example. Many people believe it is a lucky number. The ancient Pythagoreans believed seven was a special number; after all, a person has seven holes in their head, there were seven planets, etc. The number seven appears in many places in the Judeo-Christian Bible. In many cultures around the world, seven is considered a special number. Among the Cherokees, there are many examples of the importance of the number seven. There are seven clans, the council house is built with seven sides, the sacred fire is built with seven different kinds of wood, the ceremonial black drink was mixed from seven different plants, there are seven directions (east, south, north, west, up, down and here) and there are other examples. Is the prominence of the number seven in so many ancient cultures around the world, cultures that had no communication with one another, merely a coincidence? I think it more likely that the number seven reflects a reality that is universal to the human experience.

Thirteen is another number that has been prominent through the ages. Some people believe it is an unlucky number and dread Friday the thirteenth. For others, thirteen is a lucky number. Jesus chose twelve disciples to make a group of thirteen. America was founded on thirteen original colonies. The ancient Aztecs developed a calendar based upon a year of 13 months that was more accurate than the calendar we use today. Thirteen has been the most prominent number in my own life.

Thirteen was a prominent number among the ancient Cherokees. A legend is told among the Cherokees that we came from an Island in the Atlantic Ocean. At that time, there were thirteen clans of the Cherokees. The Cherokees fought a great war with the black people and were defeated. The island began to shake and spew fire and the Cherokees left the island in boats and then the island sank beneath the ocean. They sailed to the coast of what is now Central America. Many had died on the island and during the voyage so that some clans contained very few members. So they combined some clans and reorganized into seven clans and began traveling north, searching for a homeland. They came into the land of the "Fierce Ones"[7] who fought with such ferocity that the Cherokees were forced to turn toward the east. They traveled east, then north until they

_____

[7] Possibly the Mound Builders at Spiro on the Arkansas River.

settled in the area near where Ohio is today. Then, they were driven south by the Delawares until they came to the beautiful Mountains of the Blue Smoke, Sagonige (Sah-goe-nee-gay), in what is now the southeastern United States, where they established the homeland of our people.

Today, at the traditional stomp dances, the women wear leg shackles made from turtle shell rattles which provide the rhythmic beat to which the dancers dance and sing. The shackle for each leg is made with thirteen turtle shells to honor the original thirteen clans of the Cherokees.

If you enjoy the mystical significance of numbers, as I do, you might think about the sequence of numbers first pointed out by an Italian mathematician and mystic named Fibonacci. The sequence goes: 1, 1, 2, 3, 5, 8, 13, 21, 34, etc. After the beginning ones, each succeeding number is the sum of the preceding two numbers. Scholars have found that this sequence and the proportions between the numbers is related to many things in Nature, and the way the human mind perceives Nature and applies it through art, architecture, etc. The spiral of seed scales on a pine cone, the spiral of a snail's shell, perhaps the spiral of a galaxy and the spiral of a DNA molecule, the shape of a playing card, the shapes used in beautiful buildings; many of such things are related to this sequence of numbers[8].

I believe that each of us constantly receives messages from Nature and the Spirit World. Some people listen more closely and hear those messages more clearly than do most people. Among the Cherokees and other tribes of Native Americans as

---

[8] Two of the hidden meanings in the Shaman's Song in the previous chapter are that there are seven stanzas and the syllables per line, in each stanza, follow Fibonacci's sequence of 1, 2, 3, 5, 8 and 13.

well as primitive people around the world, those "careful listeners" became the Shamans and Medicine People for their tribes. The fact that much of the knowledge passed down by those people, such as the numbers I have discussed, was similar throughout the world is evidence that those things are not just coincidence but reflect a spiritual or physical reality that we do not yet understand.

You might ask, "Even if it is true, what good is it?" I believe it is possible that a greater understanding of the human mind and the psychic connections between the human mind, Nature and the Spirit World can enable us to do things that most people today would consider impossible. We read or hear about people in the past who could heal with a touch, travel outside their body, mentally communicate with others over time and space, know the future, etc. What if each of us has the capacity to do those things but just don't know how?

Sadly, for us all, the Shamans and Medicine People who might have taught us those secrets are gone; they and their wisdom were victims of the brutal conquest by insensitive invaders and intolerant religion. Let us hope that the spirits who revealed those secrets to the People of the Spirit long ago will, someday, reveal those secrets to us.

CHAPTER 8
THE LEVELS OF SPIRITUAL BEING

During the year of 2001, I began to see signs that another spiritual change was occurring in my life. Such change was not new to me, in fact, I have experienced such changes several times during my life. One, when I was a youth, involved a vision of a white bear and another, a few years ago, involved thirteen white herons and thirteen blue herons. For Native Americans, such spiritual changes often involve the appearance of a spirit bird, mammal, or other creature. I learned to accept the changes as natural events which I had no need to fear, and which I would come to understand as time passed.

As I walked on the morning of September 8, 2001, an orange butterfly brought me an understanding of the spiritual changes in my life. I am sharing them with you because I believe the plan is the same for every person. There are thirteen levels, like stair-steps, of spiritual being for persons on this earth. Basically, the steps represent spiritual growth to higher levels of spiritual awareness.

Each of the steps can be defined by certain characteristics that emerge within the person as he or she moves up to the next step. The characteristics of all thirteen levels have not been precisely revealed to me, but I will tell you about those that have been revealed to me.

A newborn baby begins life at step zero, that is, with no spiritual awareness, only physical awareness. He or she wants only to be held, fed and kept comfortable. Step one is the earliest stirrings of spiritual awareness in the form of wonder at the sight, sound, taste, and feel of the environment. Everything is new and wonderful. Step two is often related to childhood fantasies and fairy tales. At this level, the child experiences more of the feelings of enchantment and wonder that always accompany spiritual awareness.

The third step is the level of religious awareness, a belief in God, and the number relating to it is three. The significance of the trinity in the Christian religion is not a coincidence. To the feelings of enchantment and wonder the child experienced at level two are added the feelings of awe at the realization of the power of God, and feelings of trust that God will protect him or her.

For some people, the third step is the extent of their spiritual growth. During the remainder of their lives, they never feel the need to move beyond religious awareness. But, some people continue to grow beyond religious awareness to higher levels of spiritual awareness. Each higher step does not replace the steps below, but adds new dimensions to the lower steps. Thus, religion is not replaced by the steps above, but is expanded and enriched.

I was thirteen years old when I reached my fourth step and the White Bear appeared to me in a dream, and showed me my Spirit Path. As I moved to step five during my adolescence and young adulthood, I became increasingly aware of the spiritual aspects of Nature and good, wise people, particularly Cherokee Elders such as my mentor, Kawaya. They told me that the spirits would speak to me through Nature and my inner voice if I would only listen. I became increasingly aware of my own inner voice and learned to trust my intuition. I became absorbed in reading philosophy, particularly Emerson, Thoreau, Maslow and the Bible. I read those writings not only to learn, but often found verification for things that came to me through my inner voice.

As I moved to step six, I became increasingly aware of communications from the Spirit World, primarily through contact with Nature, but often from something I read or during a conversation. When I needed the answer to a question, it would appear before me, often on the page where I would open a book.

The seventh step holds special significance. The fact that the number seven had significance in the Cherokee culture, as well as many cultures around the world, including Judeo-Christian writings, is not a coincidence. At the seventh level, the person's spiritual life has grown to share equal importance with their physical life. This is the level that was the goal of the ancient Cherokee. This was the level of "Yvwi", the Real Person or Human Being. For a person who reaches the seventh level, the Spirit World has become a source of comfort, wisdom and power in every moment and every aspect of his or her life. The spirits and Nature all rush to do the bidding of the Yvwi.

My advance to the seventh step, a few years ago, was marked by the sight of thirteen white herons and thirteen blue herons around a spring fed pond one misty morning. I believe they signified a balance between my spiritual being and my physical being; the white herons representing the spiritual and the blue herons the physical.

At the seventh step, I experienced an increased ability to perceive communications from the Spirit World, and I found that my powers to make things happen increased. Young children, dogs, women, and some men, whom I would meet for the first time, seemed to instantly recognize me, like an old friend. People I had not met, but who read my writings wrote to me that it seemed I wrote directly to them and knew their thoughts. A typical example is a man from Pennsylvania who wrote, "While I am not a Native American, I find myself drawn very close and a part of the many things you choose to write about. Sometimes I feel you write about me, the way I feel about life and the world around me".

Among the ancient Cherokees, those who moved above the seventh level became the Medicine People and Shamans and their wisdom and power grew in proportion to the level they attained. All the levels are increasingly related to good, and the power for good increases with each level. Some of the powers attained by the Medicine People were: the ability to communicate with the Spirit World and the spirits of all living things; the power to heal a person's spirit or their body; control of their bodies, spirits, time and space, enabling them to travel from their bodies to other places, change into animals, birds or other creatures, bring rain or the return of the game animals or fish, and perform feats of magic.[9]

Occasionally, a rare individual, blessed by the spirits, rose to the thirteenth level, with wisdom and powers beyond human comprehension, and he or she was called Adawehi (Ah-dah-way-hee; Magician).

---

[9] Such descriptions of Spiritual power are not limited to Cherokee folklore; the Judeo-Christian Bible contains many such descriptions.

32

They were the guardians of The People. Sometimes, the Adawehi did not die. If they advanced above the thirteenth step, they moved bodily from the physical world into the Spirit World.

I have few details about the levels above seven, such as, which powers appear at which levels. With all the levels I have attained, up through seven, I have deduced the details in retrospect. However, I have neither received a powerful sign, nor developed any new powers to indicate that I have advanced above level seven. I can't describe the higher levels until I experience them.

Many years ago, when I was a boy, I once asked Kawaya if he was a Medicine Man. He replied, "That is what some people say." Not satisfied, I persisted, "But, what do **you** say you are?" He answered, "I am Yvwi."

After following my Spirit Path all these years, I believe I can also say that I am "Yvwi". It is an honorable position and a worthy goal for a Cherokee. I will continue to follow my Spirit Path and, if it is the will of the spirits, perhaps someday, I will attain a higher level of spiritual awareness and being.

CHAPTER 9
STEPS TOWARD A BETTER LIFE

In the early 1970's, my wife, Frankie, and I left high paying professional positions in Ft. Lauderdale, Florida to return to the Cherokee Nation in Oklahoma. Our inner voices told us that we should live and rear our four children close to Nature, and among our people. We built our house on the bank of the Illinois River and put our trust in the spirits. We learned to measure success not in terms of money, but in terms of fulfillment and peace. The ultimate test of any philosophy is whether or not it works. Now, thirty years later, our children are all good people with children of their own and Frankie and I are still in love, growing, busy and happy. We offer our life as testament to the truth of the words I write here.

Many people, through the ages, have attempted to describe a Beautiful Path to a fulfilling, peaceful life. I have always wanted to make a list of the steps that, in my opinion, would lead toward such a life. I wanted to write these years ago, for the benefit of my children, but I got busy and never did. The children turned out all right in spite of my procrastination. Perhaps that is evidence that it is more important to live your ideals than to write them down. Anyway, perhaps now I can make the list for my grandchildren. Most of these steps involve turning your perception and your thoughts away from the man-made world around you, and turning them inward to discover the Spirit World.

Turn off your TV and cancel your newspaper.

Most of us are very busy and wish there were more hours in the day to spend with family or on things we enjoy doing. We wonder how our grandparents had time to go on picnics or sit on the porch and visit, although, they did not have the "labor

35

saving devices" we have today. One answer is that they didn't have TV. Most of us can gain many hours each week by turning off the TV. If we do, we will gain not only time, but peace of mind. The overwhelming message on TV, and especially in the news related programs, is negative and fills us with a sense of foreboding. The same is true for newspapers, their message is predominantly violent crime, tragedy and the worst of human behavior. Their "news" is selected food for gossip mongers and the fearful. In most newspapers, the only part worth reading is the comics. Laughter is good for the soul.

Pay as you go.

Easy credit, and especially credit cards, have made us a nation of debtors with debtor mentalities. Most of us are constantly juggling our income to cover our debts, often deciding who must be paid and who can be put off for awhile. This raises our stress level and leads us toward dishonesty. It becomes a part of our thinking to the point that we find ourselves juggling everything in addition to our money, that is, our time, our commitments and our responsibilities. We neglect our responsibilities to our family and friends, putting them off to "pay" someone else.

The way out of this trap is to pay as you go. You must be wise and not take on more debt, financial or otherwise, than you can pay. Also, you must pay every debt. For example, the person who constantly takes unfair advantage of others thinks that he or she is gaining an advantage in life. But every unfair advantage carries a debt and Nature and the spirits will not tolerate imbalance. They demand that every debt be paid, one way or another. I am not saying that you will pay the debts in the hereafter; you will pay them, one way or another, during your lifetime. You can pay down your debt by giving of yourself. The spirits work through mankind and

36

Nature, so, when you help your fellow man, you do the spirits' work.

Move out of the city.

The crowded, noisy, polluted cities are not agreeable to our natures and cause sickness in our bodies and spirits. Nature holds the medicine we need. If you doubt this, look at the number of people who escape from the city to the mountains, forests or beaches for their vacations. If possible, you should live where you have close and frequent contact with Nature. Regarding closeness to Nature, the suburbs are better than the city, a small town is better than the suburbs, a house in the country is better than a small town, a tipi is better than a house, and a clean, dry cave is better than a tipi.

Most people let economic factors determine where they live. They sacrifice their independence, their peace of mind and, often, their principles in pursuit of money. But, I have found that we tend to spend what we make, whether it be much or little, and an increase in income does not automatically bring a better quality of life. Money should be near the bottom of the list of factors that determine where you live.

Live among people you like.

Frankie and I have lived in many places around the United States. Each was beautiful in one or several ways, such as, snow capped mountains, pristine forests, high deserts, rugged seacoasts, great hunting or fishing, high paying jobs, etc. But, we moved back and made our home in the Cherokee Nation of Oklahoma. Oklahoma has quiet beauty, but, its greatest beauty is it's people. Because of the people, we chose to make Oklahoma our home, and the place to rear our children.

This is not to imply that I advocate intolerance. It is desirable to live among people you like, but you must also practice tolerance and respect for those who are different from you. I believe that the same spirits are present in all living things. I have observed nothing in my experience or in history to indicate that the spirits or Nature favors any group or sect of mankind more than another or, for that matter, favors mankind over other living things. Therefore, I believe that all people and all living things deserve our respect.

Find your talent and use it.

Our goal should be to discover our talent and use it; preferably as our life's work, but at least, as a pastime. Each of us does something that is natural and easy for us, but is difficult for others. Therein lies our path to success. But often, we are afraid to pursue our talent because we feel that our talent is unimportant, that other people who have that talent are better at it than we are, or that the world will not accept us.

You must believe in yourself and be bold. You will discover that mighty forces of Nature and the Spirit World will come to your aid. You will discover that you are able to accomplish things that you have previously thought impossible. As for the acceptance of your talent by others, you will find that the world will allow you whatever position you claim. Most "special people" are only special because they had the courage to do what they feared they could not do.

Know yourself.

Most people join a church, political party or social group because their parents, friends or other influential persons convince them to do so. Then, they form their convictions based upon the convictions of their associates.

You must do exactly the opposite. Look within your self and see what your intuition will reveal to you. Those intuitions, along with your own experience, will form your convictions. Then, if you need associations, seek those that are compatible with your convictions.

Self examination is difficult and requires courage. Self-doubt is the greatest obstacle you must overcome. You are surrounded by those who think they know what is best for you. Listen to them, but let your intuition judge the truth of their words.

Seeking to know yourself is the beginning of wisdom, peace, fulfillment, and an understanding of God[10].

Trust your intuition.

Seek God within yourself and in Nature. God speaks to you through your intuition. Your intuition is your infallible guide to what is right and wrong for you.

You might think that, if every person followed their own intuition as to right and wrong rather than following a standard list composed by some religion, there would be nothing but chaos with no two people agreeing on what is right or wrong. But, right and wrong are not arbitrary rules that someone has listed. They reflect reality and truth.

I am always amazed at how the minds of people run in similar channels, regardless of how far apart they are separated by geographic location, race, creed, age, or time. What I consider beautiful or good, I find is also considered beautiful or good by many others throughout the world and over all of human history. Often, I read the words that someone wrote long before I was born and recognize a thought I had yesterday. The spirits spoke to that person and

---

[10] The totality of all spirits is the Eternal One, or God. Everything has a spirit, which is part of God.

39

spoke the same thought to me. You need not fear that your intuition will take you away from others; the intuitions of individuals are not divergent; they are parallel.

Be willing to learn.
Will Rogers, who was Cherokee, said that he never met a man he didn't like. I have met a few men, and a few women, that I didn't like, but, I never met a person from whom I couldn't learn something. Learning is my greatest source of fulfillment. I believe that learning is a lifelong process, and when a person stops learning, they begin to die.

Obviously, you can't learn everything, so, how do you determine what you should learn, and what you should ignore. In school, your teacher tells you what you should learn, but, we all know that, as soon as the course is over, we promptly forget most of what we "learned."

It used to worry me that I might forget things that I needed. But, I learned over the years that some mechanism within my mind filtered out and kept the things I needed, and discarded that which I did not need. Much more important than memorizing facts is learning how to ask the right questions, how to investigate, how to find the facts you need, and how to reach logical conclusions based on the information available.

Simplify.
The complexities of our modern world are a crushing burden to each of us. They raise our stress level to the extent of adversely affecting our mental and physical health, and shortening our lives. Our material possessions, to a large extent, add to our burden.

If you are to have peace, you must simplify your life. You must rid yourself of your excess material possessions that hang, like a great weight, around your neck. The most difficult task is determining what are necessities, and what is excess. We need to shed the excess, like a crayfish must shed its exoskeleton before it can grow.

Do what is right and do not do what is wrong.
A good life is largely a matter of choosing to do what is right, and not doing what is wrong. How do you know right from wrong? Organized religions would like you to believe they alone can define right and wrong. But, there are spiritual laws as surely as there are physical laws of the universe, and those spiritual laws are available to every person. What you, through your intuition, and other persons, through theirs, perceive as good is good. Good is related to truth, beauty, love, peace, enlightenment and fulfillment. It is not imaginary; it is as real as any matter, energy or force in the universe. It is not only good, it is right in that it is agreeable to your constitution. It is not a burden or a sacrifice but as easy, pleasant and natural as the air you breath. Finally, the greatest test of whether something is good is whether or not it works for you without harming others.

Preserve the integrity of your mind.
Throughout your life, you are surrounded by those who claim to know what is best for you. When you are a child, you need the guidance of your parents and other elders. But, when you become an adult, your mind must have independence if you are to find peace and fulfillment. Give control of your mind to no one or no thing: neither friend nor foe; neither parent nor spouse nor child; neither god nor mammon, nor church, nor political party, nor drug, nor any other thing that threatens the independence of your mind.

41

For, if you keep your mind open, you will have direct access to all you need for a happy, successful, fulfilling life. The spirits and Nature speak to mankind through open minds.

Practice moderation.
Most of our problems result from excesses. As an individual person, your mental and physical health depends upon an internal balance being maintained in your body. Excesses disrupt your internal balance. Things that are good, if used in moderation, often become bad when used in excess. Food is good and necessary, but if you eat too much, you may become obese and, usually, develop associated mental and physical problems. Behavioral excesses can also cause problems. We have all seen the bad effects of greed, hate, lust, political and religious fanaticism, etc. on the lives of individuals and those around them.

Excesses also cause most of the problems of mankind as a whole. Excessive usage of our natural resources threaten our environment and the future of mankind. Excessive political and religious fanaticism have caused countless wars and unimaginable human suffering and continue to do so. Lust for power has enslaved countless bodies and minds through the ages.

But, there are some things in which the practice of moderation is seldom necessary. Loving, practicing tolerance of those who are different from you, seeking truth, learning, helping others who need your help, enjoying and communing with Nature, and spending time with your family are all activities that it would be difficult for you to do in excess.

Seek truth and beauty.
Scientific truth, which deals primarily with the physical universe, is not constant, but changes as

new facts cause a change in the interpretation of a body of scientific knowledge.

Spiritual truth, which deals with the Spirit World, is constant, and does not change, although, the interpretations of the various religions have changed over time. Some church leaders have claimed they have the God-given and exclusive right to interpret spiritual truth, which is beyond the understanding of their followers. But, spiritual truth is simple, not complicated or mysterious. God speaks to every person, and spiritual truth is revealed to any person who seeks it with a pure heart and an open mind. Every healthy mind recognizes spiritual truth.

Through your life, choose to walk a Beautiful Path and let beauty become your way of life. Beauty gives pleasure to your senses and exalts your mind and spirit. Inherent in beauty is a sense of truth, peace, completeness, balance and suitability. Beautiful things or experiences are a good fit; they are just right. Beauty, so defined, is the best word I know to express the mystic harmony which exists among the Spirit World, Nature, and your own spirit.

One of my favorite poems is a Benedictory Chant from the Navahos. It ends with the lines:

Beauty is before me
And beauty behind me,
Above and below me hovers the beautiful,
I am surrounded by it,
I am immersed in it.
In my youth I am aware of it,
And in old age
I shall walk quietly
The beautiful trail.

The poem is Navaho, but it also describes the life of a Cherokee who walks the Cherokee Spirit Path. I have shared with you some things I have

learned as I have walked my Spirit Path. I tell you
these things to encourage you to seek your own Spirit
Path. I have provided you with some guidelines that
can help you on your journey. I believe it is a journey
infinitely worth taking. "Walking in beauty" is not an
exaggeration or fantasy, but is completely true and
possible for you.

MY SPIRIT PATH

I am at peace.
I believe that I am doing
That which I am supposed to do,
Living where I am supposed to live,
In the time that is supposed to be.

The Eternal One had a purpose for me
Or It would not have sent my spirit
Into this body
In this place
In this time.

In my youth,
The Eternal One showed me a Spirit Path
Which I chose to follow.
On my Path, I have met
Many wise spirits
Who taught me,
Many kind spirits
Who loved me,
Many blithe spirits
Who laughed with me.
Now, beauty surrounds me.
The spirits   protect me.
I am at   peace.

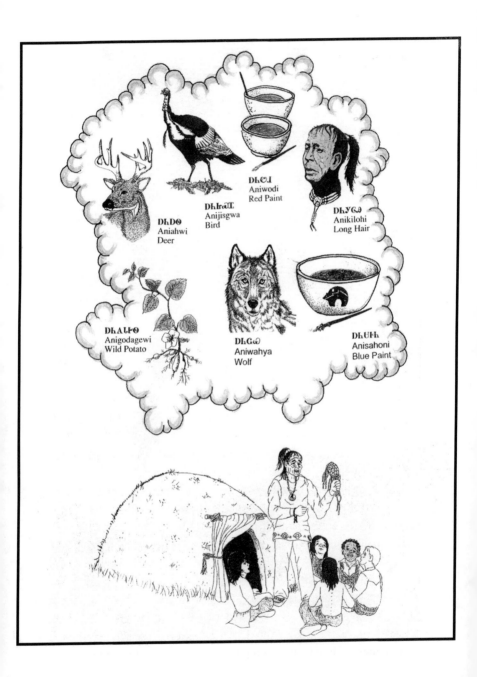

ᎠᏂᎠᏫ
Aniahwi
Deer

ᎠᏂᏥᏍᏆ
Anijisgwa
Bird

ᎠᏂᏬᏗ
Aniwodi
Red Paint

ᎠᏂᎩᎶᎯ
Anikilohi
Long Hair

ᎠᏂᎪᏓᎨᏫ
Anigodagewi
Wild Potato

ᎠᏂᏩᏯ
Aniwahya
Wolf

ᎠᏂᏌᎰᏂ
Anisahoni
Blue Paint

CHAPTER 10
THE CHEROKEE CLANS

The seven clans of the Cherokees are: Aniwahya (Ah-nee-wah-hyah; Wolf Clan), Anisahoni (Ah-nee-sah-hoe-nee; Blue Clan), Aniahwi (Ah-nee-ah-hwee; Deer Clan), Aniwodi (Ah-nee-woe-dee; Paint Clan), Anijisgwa (Ah-nee-jee-sgwah; Bird Clan), Anikilohi (Ah-nee-kee-loe-hee; Long Hair Clan), and Anigodagewi (Ah-nee-goe-dah-gay-wee; Wild Potato Clan). I will tell you some things about each clan, and in particular, the Anikilohi, which is my clan.

The Aniwahya, Wolf Clan, was the largest clan. In the olden days, it was the warrior clan and they were the guardians of the tribe. Of course, in time of war, men, and some women, from all clans fought, but the men of the Wolf Clan might be thought of as the "Special Forces" of the Cherokees. The males were trained from boyhood for warfare. They served as guards around the walled towns. A guard who fell asleep or otherwise failed in his duty was condemned and then publicly brained with a club in the center of town. Members of the Wolf Clan were the first to enter the stomp dance arena and they sat on the south side of the circle. The War Chief usually came from this clan. The War Chief wore a robe of red feathers. Members of this clan were the only Cherokees allowed to kill a wolf. Also known as the Earth People, they were skilled pipe makers and potters.

The Anisahoni, Blue Clan, was sometimes called Blue Paint Clan and, sometimes, Wildcat Clan. In the olden days, this was Aniyoni (Ah-nee-yoe-nee; Bear Clan). These were known as the builders of houses, town walls, granaries, and the dome shaped osi (oh-see), which was used as a sweat lodge and a winter sleeping room. I was told that the members of this clan excelled in the making of bows, arrows and other weapons and tools. They were also medicine people for the children of the tribe.

The Aniahwi, Deer Clan, was called Anikawi (Ah-nee-kah-wee) in olden days. These were the "keepers[11]" of the deer and some clan members were able to communicate with the deer. Members of this clan were known as skilled makers of clothing. They were also known as skilled hunters and fast runners.

The Aniwodi, Paint Clan, sometimes called Red Paint Clan, was called Aninvwoti (Ah-nee-nuh-woe-tee; Medicine Clan) in olden days. They were the keepers of the ancient medicinal secrets and gatherers of medicinal herbs. Sorcerers and medicine men and women came mainly from this clan.

Members of the Anijisqwah, Bird Clan, were the keepers of the birds. The Cherokees had semi-domesticated turkeys and also kept, as pets and/or decoys, pigeons, parrots, crows, geese, ducks and

---

[11]The term "keepers" could imply a physical keeping or tending of something or a spiritual tending of something in the wild, as in this case, the wild deer.

48

probably other birds. Some members of this clan could communicate with the Spirit World through wild birds or by turning into birds. They were also the messengers for the tribe, running with messages between towns in the vast Cherokee Nation.

The Anigodagewi, Wild Potato Clan was sometimes called "Blind Savannah Clan". They were skilled farmers and keepers of the land. These tasks were performed by the women of all the clans, but, the women of the Wild Potato Clan were specialists. They were also skilled at finding and digging wild potatoes. The men of this clan organized and officiated at games such as stickball, chungke and cornstalk shooting. Many of them were skilled stick-ball players.

The Anikilohi, Long-Hair Clan, was called Anikilo (Ah-nee-kee-loe; Stranger Clan) in olden days. They were the teachers, priests and keepers of the ancient lore. They taught the aliens or adopted persons how to be Aniyvwiya, and then the aliens became members of this clan. The Peace Chief usually came from this clan and wore a robe of white feathers. The old name, Anikilo or "Strangers" came from the fact that many members of this clan were not of Cherokee blood or were mixed blood; their mothers being non-Cherokee. The men did not shave their heads as did the Cherokee warriors of other clans; thus the name "long-hair". They sought peace rather than war.

The Anikilohi is my clan. There are several unusual facts about the Long Hair Clan that, in my opinion, provide an insight into the social structure as well as the mind of the early Cherokees. I believe the people of today's world, including some Cherokees, can learn from the ancient Anikilohi.

The name "Stranger Clan" referred to the fact that non-Cherokee strangers, captives, runaway slaves and others adopted into the tribe became members of this clan. Some were not of Cherokee blood and others were of Cherokee blood only on their father's side. Since clan membership was determined by the mother's clan membership, children born to a Cherokee father but a non-Cherokee mother, could become members of the Long Hair Clan.

The members of the Long Hair Clan were the teachers and keepers of the ancient Cherokee wisdom and taught a newcomer how to be Yvwi (Yuh-wee; true person, human being, Cherokee). It is very interesting to me that this clan was entrusted with these vital responsibilities. It is as if the ancient Cherokees were wise enough to realize that, often, strangers can see us more clearly than we can see ourselves.

The White or Peace Chief, who wore a robe of white feathers and wielded great influence in the tribe, usually came from the Long Hair Clan. Thus a person who was of mixed Cherokee blood or perhaps no Cherokee blood at all could become a Chief. I think the ancient Cherokees could teach many of today's people a few things about the value of tolerance and diversity to a society. They knew that what is in a person's heart is more important than degree of blood, skin color or any of the other superficial features by which many people judge others.

There are, presently, about 240,000 enrolled members of the Western Cherokee Nation. There are many thousands of others, living all over the United States, who are of Cherokee descent who want to become members of the Cherokee Nation but cannot because they cannot trace their lineage back to an enrolled Cherokee. Because their heroic ancestors escaped the white man's round-up, enrollment and removal of the Cherokees, these descendents are denied their identity as Cherokees. They are denied their identity by the Federal

Government, but more tragically, by the Cherokee Nation itself.

The ancient Cherokees, the "Real People", would have welcomed these people who, in their hearts, are Cherokee. Perhaps, some day, the modern-day Cherokee Nation will find a way for these people to join us. The procedure for a person becoming a member of the ancient Long Hair Clan had some similarities with today's procedure for a foreign person becoming a citizen of the United States. Perhaps, to become a citizen of the Cherokee Nation today, a person could be required to live within the Cherokee Nation for a few years, study the Cherokee language, history, culture and laws, and take an oath of allegiance to the Cherokee Nation. They would then be granted citizenship in the Cherokee Nation, just as were the ancient Anikilohi.

In the Beginning

In the beginning was God, the Eternal One; the totality of all spirits in One.

God said, "Let us create a garden for us to inhabit." So, the spirits of the stones created the earth, the sun, the moon and the stars. The spirits of the waters created the seas, the lakes and the rivers. The spirits of the air created the atmosphere. The spirits of the fire created fire and the light and heat of the sun, the earth and the stars. Each spirit dwelled within the thing that it had created. God looked upon the earth, the sun, the moon, the stars, the waters, the atmosphere, and the light and heat, and saw that they were good.

God said, "Let us put living things in our garden. Let every spirit create a living thing to inhabit, and that living thing shall be in the image of that spirit." So, the spirits of the animals created the animals, and the spirits of the plants created the plants, each in its own image. Each spirit dwelled within the animal or the plant that it had created. God looked upon the animals and the plants and saw that they were good, and each spirit looked upon the garden, and saw that it was beautiful.

God said, "Let us establish laws for the governing of our garden." So, the spirits established laws to govern the earth, the waters, the air and the fire. The spirits of the animals and the plants established laws to govern all the living things. God looked upon the laws and saw that they were good, and each spirit looked upon the laws, and saw that they were true.

Thus, God created the garden we call earth and all that is within it. God saw that everything that had been created, and the laws that govern them, and the spirits that live within them, are all good and beautiful and true.

CHAPTER 11
THE ANCIENT CHEROKEE RELIGION

When I was a boy growing up in the Cherokee Nation of Oklahoma, I heard the Elders talk of the days long ago, before the white man came. Of course, none of them actually remembered those days because the white man came long before any of them were born. But they repeated old stories that they had heard as children from their elders, who had heard them from their elders and so on back through the generations to the olden days.

There were also some relatives and friends who showed me written documents of early Cherokee life, written in the Cherokee characters invented by Sequoyah, that had been passed down through their families. Some of those documents were letters between sweethearts, some were records of business dealings, some were records of tribal government, and some were entire books of myths, sacred formulas, and medicinal practices that had been carefully recorded by the Shamans who practiced them in their daily lives. Those wise people foresaw that the ancient wisdom would be lost to the advancement of civilization if it was not recorded.

The ancient Cherokee cosmology consisted of a Spirit World and a Physical World. In the Spirit World, there dwelt the archetypes of all the things in the Physical World. These archetypes were not merely spirit images of the physical things, but were much greater, as in the Judeo-Christian religion, man was made in God's image, but God is much greater than man.

Thus, in the ancient Cherokee religion, the archetype of the bears was the White Bear, the archetype of the deer was Little Deer, and so on for each group of animals, birds, insects, fish, etc. and to a lesser extent for plants. The people prayed to the archetypes for favors and the Shamans invoked the archetypes by special ceremonies. The animal archetypes were the most often invoked, with insects and fishes occupying a subordinate place. The four-legged animals, birds and reptiles were invoked almost constantly. In ceremonies conducted by the Shamans, the most frequently invoked animal archetypes were the dog, the squirrel, the rabbit, various hawks, the box turtle and the rattlesnake.

Humans were not considered to be above the other animals in importance. One archetype of mankind was the Red Man or the Red Woman.

Above all these were the elemental archetypes, the principal of which were fire, water and the sun. The sun archetype was called Unehlanvhi (Oo-nay-hlah-nuh-hee; Apportioner of All Things). Early Christian missionaries mistakenly believed this to be the Cherokee "Great Spirit[12]", and used the term as a synonym for "God" in their translations of the Bible. Among the ancient Cherokees, prayers were often directed to Unehlanvhi, particularly by players of stickball.

The water archetype was Yvwi Ganvhida (Yuh-wee Gah-nuh-hee-dah; Long Person) and refers to the river. Virtually every important ceremony, whether connected to the stickball game, hunting, medicine or love contained a prayer to Yvwi Ganvhida. The House of the Shaman was Amayuldi (ah-mah-yule-dee; by the river), because that was a sacred place.

The fire archetype was actually two; Ajila Gigage (Ah-jee-lah Gee-gah-gay; Red Fire) and Ajila Unega (Ah-jee-lah Oo-nay-gah; White Fire). The color of fire invoked depended upon the need. For example, the Ancient White (White Fire) was invoked by the Shaman to drive fish, turtles, or snakes, which were causing illness, from the body of the patient. The hunter prayed to the Ancient Red (Red Fire) and the Ancient White for good omens of success on the coming hunt.

Before a stomp dance, the sacred fire was kindled in the center of the dance circle. In times of peace, the White Paths, which stretched east to west and south to north to the ends of the earth and signified peace and happiness, were said to cross at the sacred fire. The fire which was kindled in preparation for war was said to be the crossing point for the Red Paths, which signified success and triumph.

James Mooney, who extensively and scientifically observed the Cherokees from 1887 to

---

[12] I believe the Cherokee "Great Spirit" to be the totality of all spirits and I call it Sagwu Igohidv (Sah-gwoo Ee-goe-hee-duh; Eternal One).

1890, wrote of our ancient religion in his reports to the Bureau of American Ethnology. He stated[13]:

> The Indian is essentially religious and contemplative, and it might almost be said that every act of his life is regulated and determined by his religious belief. It matters not that some may call this superstition. The difference is only relative. When we are willing to admit that the Indian has a religion which he holds sacred, even though it may be different from our own, we can then admire the consistency of the theory, the particularity of the ceremonial and the beauty of the expression. There is a wonderful completeness about the whole system which is not surpassed even by the ceremonial religions of the East. The Cherokee Indian was a polytheist and the spirit world was to him only a shadowy counterpart of this. All his prayers were for temporal and tangible blessings--for health, for long life, for success in the chase, in fishing, in war and in love, for good crops, for protection and for revenge. He had no Great Spirit, no happy hunting ground, no heaven, no hell, and consequently death had for him no terrors and he awaited the inevitable end with no anxiety as to the future. He was careful not to violate the rights of his tribesman or to do injury to his feelings, but there is nothing to show that he had any idea whatever of what is called morality in the abstract.

---

[13] From "Sacred Formulas of the Cherokees" by James Mooney. For brevity, I have omitted brief portions of Mooney's statement which I felt were unnecessary to his meaning.

Of course, we must keep in mind that Mooney's background did not prepare him to fully understand the Cherokee Way, and he thus made some errors in his observations and interpretations.

For example, I strongly disagree with Mooney's last sentence in the statement above. In my opinion, the early Cherokees had a higher morality than did the European invaders who deceived, cruelly conquered and slaughtered many of us, and expelled us from our homelands. Many early observers recorded the honesty, faithfulness, and other moral qualities of the early Cherokees. Some even wrote of the "Noble Red Man", and I believe that was, generally, an accurate assessment. The Cherokee elders and parents taught the children the importance of becoming Yvwi (Yuh-wee; Human Being, Real Person), who was a good and worthy person in balance within himself or herself, with other persons and with Nature. The reward for being Yvwi came in the form of a happy and successful life, and was not postponed until the hereafter as in the Christian religion. The spirits and Nature hastened to do the bidding of the Yvwi. This belief formed the definition and the motivation for moral conduct.

Today, the majority of Cherokees embrace the Christian faith. A small minority, primarily of the Kituwa (Kee-too-wah; Nighthawk Society), still follow the ancient religion. Many Cherokees believe that Christianity and the ancient Cherokee religion are compatible, and they draw comfort and wisdom from both. Regardless of the current religious beliefs of the Cherokees, the ancient religion remains an important part of the heritage of every Cherokee. Our heritage, more than any other factor, determines who we are.

CHAPTER 12
CHEROKEE STOMP GROUNDS

With the arrival of the white man in the new world came the Christian Missionaries, bringing their faith to the Native Americans. As part of the conversion of the Native Americans to Christianity, their traditional religious practices were discouraged, and their religious structures and artifacts were often destroyed. With the Cherokees, as with most tribes of Native Americans, the missionaries did their job well. Today, and for the past 100 years, the majority of Cherokees belong to the Christian faith.

However, there remains a residue of the "Old Ways" among most Cherokees, regardless of degree of Cherokee blood, religious background, educational level or socioeconomic status. For many Cherokees, the Stomp Ground remains a sacred place. Many Cherokees who regularly attend Christian church services still attend and participate in dances and ceremonies at Stomp Grounds. They do not consider the traditional beliefs an alternative to Christianity, but a supplement to it with the same goals. For other Cherokees, who do not profess the Christian faith, their Stomp Ground may be their only church.

The Stomp Ground, as a Cherokee center for religious and social activity, probably dates back to pre-Columbian times, although, the details of its beginning are no longer known. The Keetoowah or Nighthawk Society of the Cherokee is generally considered the religious arm of the Cherokees. They have been responsible for establishing and maintaining stomp grounds and conducting ceremonies. In 1859, a set of by-laws defining the physical requirements of the stomp ground were first written down by Keetoowah leaders.

The by-laws call for a centrally located Sacred Fire surrounded by an open area for dancing, and this area is surrounded by seven arbors facing inward. The by-laws, also, call for a council house, medicine fire, a cooking and meeting arbor, a water-well or spring, and a stickball field.

Stomp dances are typically held at the site two or three times each year to commemorate major Cherokee holidays. The largest of the year is held on Labor Day weekend when several hundred people gather and camp at the site for several days. It is a time for renewing old acquaintances, singing, dancing, celebrating life and paying tribute to the Eternal One.

The Sacred Fire serves as the center for all ceremonies, songs and dances, prayers, and sermons. The Sacred Fire is built on a flat-topped mound of earth about six feet across at the top. First, four logs about a foot in diameter and eighteen inches long are placed on the mound with their ends toward the center and their other ends pointing south, north, west and east. These mark the place of crossing of the White Paths which reach to the ends of the earth. The Sacred Fire is then kindled in the center of the mound.

The circular area around the Sacred Fire is about twenty yards wide, and during the stomp dances the participants sing and dance in a counterclockwise circle. The only instruments allowed are a small drum for setting the rhythm, and turtle-shell shackles worn on the ankles of some women that rattle as the women dance. Thirteen turtle shells, each containing small pebbles, make up each shackle and one shackle is worn on each ankle.

Equally spaced around the dance area are the seven arbors or huts, one for each of the seven clans. Directly to the south of the Sacred Fire is the arbor of the Wolf Clan. Counterclockwise, next to it is the arbor of the Blue Clan, then Deer Clan, Paint Clan, Bird Clan, Long Hair Clan, and Wild Potato Clan in that order around the circle. The arbors were typically constructed of poles to form a platform roof which was then covered with leafy branches to provide shade and protection from dew or light rain, although, now roofs are usually made of tin. There are benches in each arbor for members of the clan.

The medicine fire is kindled outside the circle of the Sacred Fire, often within a structure, such as the Council House. Medicine kettles are kept simmering over the fire to which Medicine Men add roots and herbs in secret to produce their healing medicines. The Council House is built with seven sides with the doorway facing south.

The Stickball Field provides an area of recreation for the children, as well as, the playing of stickball. A pole about twenty feet tall with a carved wooden fish about two feet long fastened to the top is located in the middle of the field. During the stickball game, men and boys must catch and throw the small ball with two sticks, each about two feet long with a small, netted hoop at the end. Women and girls can catch and throw the ball with their hands. In the old days, as many as a hundred people might be on each team and play was very rough; sometimes more like war than sport. Today, players are asked to exercise restraint so that sometimes even small children play on the teams. The ball is thrown at the fish, and seven points are awarded for hitting the fish or one point for hitting the pole above the mark.

The people begin arriving a day or two before the activities begin, and set up camps by families and clans in the area surrounding the Stomp Grounds. A hog or two may be donated to be butchered, and the meat distributed among the people.

The official ceremonies begin with the lighting of the Sacred Fire and smoking the pipe to bless the grounds. The Sacred Fire is kindled by the Keeper of the Fire and his Assistant before dawn on the day when services begin. Popular belief holds that the Sacred Fire is kindled from coals of the Eternal Fire which was given to the Cherokees by the Eternal One, and was carried to Indian Territory over the Trail of Tears from the Cherokee homeland in the East. The fire is built with seven kinds of wood and is regularly replenished with wood to keep it burning night and day until the activities end. After the Sacred Fire is lit, the Keeper of the Fire and the Assistant make a sacrifice of a small piece of meat or chicken. Then they pray for guidance and smoke sacred tobacco in pipes to bless the grounds. The Stomp Ground is now a holy place, a church without walls.

During the morning, food is cooked by the women. Those who are pregnant or in their menstrual period do not participate in food preparation. Stickball is played, meetings are held and prayers are offered. At the noon meal, as with all meals involving a large number of persons, the men eat first, followed by the children and the women eat last. Customarily, each person spits out onto the ground the first bite of food they take as a token of returning to nature part of what they have received.

In the afternoon, sermons and oral history are offered around the Sacred Fire. As twilight falls, families are gathered around many small fires surrounding the Stomp Grounds, eating and visiting.

As darkness falls, the people gather around the central area and the Sacred Fire. The ancient stone pipe is lit and as each clan files into the central area, each clan member takes seven puffs on the pipe and passes it to the next person. Prayers and sermons are offered, and a collection is received to help pay for the food and for charity. An informal business meeting is held by the Chiefs, Elders, Medicine Men and other interested persons while the people patiently await the dancing.

Finally, a loud voice and shaking rattle announce the first call for dancing. After a few minutes, the second call for dancing is given and the dancers begin to assemble in the central area. The first dance is by invitation. Tribal Officers, Medicine Men, Clan Heads and Elders are the first called. A small drum sets the beat for the dance and the shell shakers take up the rhythm. The dancers begin their shuffling gait around the circle as the flames and sparks of the Sacred Fire leap toward the stars. Other people begin to join the dancing. The Lead Singer sings each ancient phrase, and the dancers sing their response in turn. The sights and sounds are truly awesome and can bring chills to your spine and tears to your eyes. The dancing continues through the night. There is no age barrier and even non-Cherokee visitors are invited to dance.

During the days and nights of activities, various ceremonies are held and the sacred Wampum Belts kept by the Keetoowah Society may be shown and interpreted in the Sermon of the Belts. The message of the Wampum Belts is a belief in the Eternal One, peace, and the love and fellowship of mankind. The Belts teach that one should follow the White Path, the way of cleanliness and balance in mind and body, and avoid the Dark Path, the way of the unclean and imbalanced. The Spirit Path is a general concept held by many pre-Columbian Native Americans as the path to becoming a true Human Being. The Cherokees call it the White Path, the Sioux call it the Red Road, and other tribes use other names but all are referring to a similar concept.

To my knowledge, there are only two active, major stomp grounds in the Cherokee Nation at the present time. They are the Redbird Smith Stomp Ground, north of Vian and the oldest in the Cherokee Nation, and the Stokes Smith Stomp Ground, south of Marble City which is the more active of the two. During stomp dances, the grounds are patrolled by Cherokee police and no alcohol, drugs or rowdiness are allowed. Non-Cherokee visitors are welcome, although, there are some restrictions on photography, recording and attendance at some ceremonies.

CHAPTER 13
RICHARD MCLEMORE

Richard McLemore made and gave me my first bow when I was a small boy. He could make almost anything from materials at hand and he had a great knowledge of nature, hunting and fishing. He learned from his Cherokee Elders and tried to pass some of his skills and knowledge to others, including me.

Richard, his wife and young son lived near the spring branch in McLemore Hollow, two or three miles from my boyhood home in the Cherokee Nation of Oklahoma. Like so many of the Cherokee Elders that I knew, Richard was a kind and gentle person who always had time to teach a young boy or girl.

As I have written previously, Kawaya was like a grandfather to me. Richard was not related to me, but he was like an uncle or even a second father to me. I loved being with Kawaya because he was wise and he taught me many things. But I also loved bows and arrows and hunting. Richard was the best bow maker and the best hunter in the community so I spent a lot of time with him.

Richard did most of his work in a small shed under a big sycamore tree in back of his house. Under the shed, he had a forge, an anvil mounted on a tree stump, and a vice mounted on a small workbench that was anchored to the big sycamore. A spring, where the family got their drinking water, ran from under a nearby ledge of rock, formed a small pool, and then ran for a short distance where it joined the spring branch. I spent many lazy summer hours in the shade watching Richard work at his forge and anvil, shaping hot metal with his hammer or shaping wood with his draw-knife.

Richard sold or bartered most of the things he made, although, he did not depend on that income for his living. He worked as a day laborer at various jobs such as picking strawberries or beans on nearby farms or working cattle on nearby ranches. Occasionally he worked on road or railroad construction or repair. He liked the freedom to work when he wanted to and to take time to do other things he enjoyed.

He was expert with many tools but, especially, the ax. He cut trees and hewed them into cross ties for the railroads with his broad ax. I once heard a story about Richard's skill with the ax which I will relate to you.

Richard heard that they were constructing a bridge a few miles from his home so he took his axes and walked to the bridge site. The boss asked Richard if he could hew two long beams (I think Richard called them "sleepers") which would support the floor of the bridge. Richard said he could do the job.

First, Richard took his broad ax to a stump where he could sit down. He took a sharpening stone from his pocket and began honing his ax. He worked on it for more than an hour until he was satisfied with the edge. Then he marked the first log with his chalk box, notched it, at intervals, with his pole ax and then began hewing with his broad ax. Those watching, many of whom were ax men themselves, were amazed at the speed and precision with which he worked. Before long, the beams were finished and were perfect. I'm not positive, but I believe the person who was telling me said the beams were each more than thirty feet long and a foot wide.

But Richard's skills that I most remember were related to the making and using of fish gigs. He made the gig heads from steel; he preferred leaf springs from a buggy or old Ford car, although, I have one gig head he made for my father from a horse-shoeing rasp. Each gig head had a socket for fitting it onto the gig pole which was usually 12 to 16 feet long and an inch in diameter, and was made from black locust wood. The gig heads were 12 to 14 inches long with two barbed prongs each about 5/16 inch thick and 5 to 6 inches long. The tips of the prongs were blunt and rounded; it was unnecessary that they be sharp to penetrate the fish. The gig was used to pole the boat as well as to gig fish.

While my father and most giggers preferred to gig at night by the light of a gas lantern while standing in the front of a john-boat, Richard preferred to gig from the bank in the daylight. He used a single pronged barbed spear, made exactly like a two pronged gig except for having only one prong. His slow movements along the creek bank reminded me of the movements of a great blue heron, and he used his spear with the same precision that a heron uses its beak. He seldom missed a fish regardless of how fast it was moving.

I realized that his skill was even more remarkable than I first thought when I first tried gigging. I discovered the fish was not where it appeared to be. The gig-pole appeared to bend at the surface of the water, and I always struck above the fish. Richard taught me that I had to aim below the fish to hit it with a gig or an arrow.

Most of the fish we gigged were rough fish such as suckers, buffalo and drum, although, an occasional bass was taken if it got careless. Rough fish, taken from clean water, have a delicious taste, but are very bony. The bones were overcome by scaling the fish, and then scoring their sides to the bone about every inch. The fish were then dipped in corn meal, salted, and fried in deep, boiling lard. Most of the small bones would cook so they could be eaten with no difficulty.

Since our house was near the creek, Richard would usually stop and get me when he was going to gig fish. Many cold winter days, we slipped along the creek bank gigging fish until we had a mess. We would clean the fish and sometimes, while we warmed ourselves by her wood cookstove, my mother would fry the fish and a skillet of fried potatoes on top of the stove, while a pan of cornbread baked in the oven. That, along with a slice of raw onion and a glass of cold buttermilk, was food fit for a Chief.

CHAPTER 14
LEARNING TO SEE

Through my life, I have been blessed to know a few remarkable people who taught me to see. Of course, being born with normal vision, I could see soon after birth, but those people taught me that I could see things beyond what most people see. Two of my teachers were the Cherokee men I have written about; Richard McLemore and Kawaya.

Richard was not kin to my family, but he became like an uncle to me. Among traditional

Cherokees, a boy's uncles, on his mother's side, taught him the skills of the hunter and other things a boy should know. My mother had no brothers to teach me the Cherokee ways, so, Richard became like an uncle to me. He made my first bow and arrows when I was about six years old. A couple of years later, when my bow broke, he told me I was old enough to make my own bow and he helped me make my first bow. He showed me how to see the grain layers in the Osage orange bow wood and follow the grain layers with his draw knife. He taught me that the draw knife sounds differently in the different layers of wood. I remember him telling me, "Listen to the wood. It will talk to you."

In the winter, Richard and I gigged fish in Barren Fork Creek and through the late spring, summer and fall, we hunted squirrels in the woods. Sometimes we hunted with a dog that would tree the squirrels and sometimes we still hunted, silently slipping through the woods looking for the squirrels. Or, sometimes, we sat still near a tree where the squirrels were coming to feed on something, like mulberries or hickory nuts, and waited for the squirrels to come.

Richard and I both enjoyed hunting, but we didn't hunt just for fun; we hunted for meat to supplement the diets of our families. So, we usually hunted with a shotgun or rifle because a gun is more efficient than a bow. Richard usually carried a .22 rifle and I carried my little .410 shotgun. If we could see the squirrel sitting still, we usually shot it with the .22, since .22 shells cost less than shotgun shells. But, if it ran, I shot it with the shotgun. Sometimes, if we didn't have ammunition for our guns, we hunted with our bows.

When I first started hunting squirrels with Richard, I was amazed by how he could spot the squirrels. Maybe the dog would tree up a big red-oak tree, sixty feet high, with huge limbs covered with leaves and a thousand places for a squirrel to hide. Richard and I would get back away from the tree, on opposite sides, and begin to circle the tree, searching the branches above with our eyes while the dog jumped and barked at the base of the tree. Richard would always spot the squirrel first. Then, he would patiently try to show me the squirrel.

"See," he might say, "there in the very top. See that dark spot in that bunch of leaves. That is the squirrel." I would see the dark spot, but it looked no different from twenty other dark spots I could see in bunches of leaves. But, when I would shoot the spot with my little shotgun, out would fall the squirrel. Or, often, the squirrel would be hugging the trunk or a big limb of the tree and would move around to the other side as I circled the tree. By the two of us circling on opposite sides of the tree, sometimes one of us could see the squirrel that was hidden from the other. Or, sometimes, Richard would tell me to shake a small tree close to where I was circling. The commotion would cause the squirrel to move around to Richard's side where he could see it and get a shot. Gradually, over the years, I learned to find the squirrels as well as Richard. In fact, I became so successful at hunting squirrels that Richard gave me the Cherokee name of Saloli (Sah-low-lee; Squirrel).

As I wrote previously, another person with whom I spent a lot of time, during my boyhood years, was an elderly Cherokee man named Kawaya. Kawaya lived alone in a cabin up Barren Fork Creek from our farm. Kawaya became like a grandfather to me. Kawaya didn't make bows or hunt, but he liked to fish, hunt for wild bee trees and gather edible or medicinal plants from the woods and fields.

In almost everything Kawaya did, there was a lesson to be learned. Sometimes I didn't pay close attention and often I didn't realize the significance of what was happening until later, sometimes years later, but Kawaya understood my mind and was patient with me.

I remember the summer night I went with Kawaya for the first time to catch crayfish to use as bait for fishing the next day. That night, I was to learn a lesson in seeing. The night was warm as we waded into the spring branch, carrying a kerosene lantern and an empty lard pail. The water was so cold it almost took away my breath and it was as clear as crystal. Kawaya told me to keep only the soft-shelled crayfish. The soft-shells were those that had recently shed their shell or exoskeleton and whose new shell had not yet hardened. He said we would also keep the "peelers", those with hard shells almost ready to be shed. The hard shell could easily be peeled off before the crayfish was put on the fishhook, and the fish liked them just as well as the soft-shells.

Crayfish stay hidden under rocks during daylight, but come out after dark. The light of the lantern showed the rocky bottom of the spring branch was infested with crayfish. Every rock on the bottom sheltered a half dozen or more and crayfish were darting and crawling everywhere in the pools. It was great fun grabbing them and Kawaya and I looked like two bears in the midst of a salmon run as we laughed and splashed.

I would catch a crayfish and feel to see if its shell was soft. Usually it wasn't, so I threw it down the branch out of the pool so I wouldn't catch it again. If it was soft, I put it in the pail. I was catching ten or more hard-shells for every soft-shell. Then I noticed that Kawaya was putting every crayfish he caught into his pail.

"Edudu (Aye-doo-doo; Grandfather)," I said, "I thought you said we were keeping only the soft-shells."

"That is true, Saloli (Sah-loe-lee; Squirrel)," he replied.

"But you are putting every one you catch into the pail."

"That is true," he said and then he smiled as he anticipated my next question. "I only catch the soft-shells and the peelers."

"But how can you tell them from the hard-shells without feeling them?" I asked.

"I would tell you how, if I could, but I don't know how to say it," he answered.

I looked and looked, but I could see no difference in the crayfish, and I told Kawaya I could see no difference.

"Saloli," he said, "You look but you do not see. My eyes are no better than yours, but I see things you do not see. But you can learn to use your eyes to see things that other people do not see."

Finally, after many crayfish catching trips, I learned to distinguish soft-shells, peelers and hard-shells by subtle differences in their appearance and actions under the water, but like Kawaya, I can't tell you how to recognize the difference.

Over the years, I learned that Kawaya and Richard were teaching me not only perception with all my senses, but seeing that goes beyond the senses. I learned that, as one lives in harmony with Nature, he or she grows in awareness, and there are many things that are perceived in ways that cannot be explained. The normal five senses become more attuned to the signals coming from Nature, but in addition, there are other perceptions that seem to be received by senses outside the normal senses. Those perceptions stimulate vague feelings or intuitions in the conscious mind, and visions or dreams in the unconscious. Those are perceptions of the spirits.

CHAPTER 15
THE FOUR SOULS

The ancient Cherokees lived in a world in which the spiritual and the physical were of equal importance. Virtually every waking moment, they were aware of the effect of the spirits on every aspect of their lives in the physical world. The spiritual beliefs of the early Cherokees were beautiful in their consistency, detail, completeness, and relevance to their lives. The concept of the four souls was one segment of their spiritual beliefs. It tied together Cherokee beliefs relating to human physiology, doctoring, conjuring, witchcraft, death and funerals.

It was believed that every person has four souls and that there are four stages of death. The souls are each referred to as Askina (Ah-skee-nah; soul, spirit or ghost).[14]

The first soul is the soul of conscious life which animates the other three souls. This soul is human, not physical, is conscious, has memory, personality,

---

[14] Before Christianity, the Cherokees had no words for devil or hell. Translators of the Bible used Askina as the word for devil or demon.

continuity after death, and is unitary in its essence. This soul is located under the top of the head, where the "soft spot" of a young baby is located. The practice of scalping is magic directed against this soul. This soul creates the watery fluids of the body such as saliva and lymph. Magical attack upon this soul by a conjuror[15] is sometimes called "spoiling his saliva." A conjuror, bent on harm, might secretly follow a person until the person spits upon the ground. The conjuror retrieves the spittle and uses it to create a magical potion or object to use against the person.

Upon the death of the person, the first soul immediately leaves the body and continues its personal life, sometimes remaining nearby for awhile, and sometimes seen as a ghost. Some say this soul eventually finds its way to the Land of the Dead in the West, and some say it goes into the river, follows it upstream to its source at a spring, where the soul then goes down into an underworld. This departed soul might continue to communicate with a loved one, still living, through a ringing in the ears of the loved one.

The second soul is the soul of physiological life. This soul is possessed by all animals, is a substance, has no individuality and is quantitative; there being more or less of it in the person or animal. This soul is located in the liver, and it creates yellow bile, black bile, and digestive juices. It is of primary importance in doctoring and conjuring, and often the target of witches. Witches strengthen themselves and lengthen their lives by drawing out the liver-soul from

---

[15] The term "medicine man (or woman)" is often seen instead of "conjuror." Conjurors and witches are basically the same, depending on whether they are for you or against you. One man's conjuror is his enemy's witch.

their victims. Conjurors can also attack this soul, producing similar effects. The effects of liver-soul depletion or destruction produces listlessness and the "yellows" (jaundice) or depression and the "black" (gall bladder attacks or pancreatitis). Exhaustion of the liver-soul substance produces death.

Upon the death of the person and the departure of the first soul, all life processes stop and the other three souls begin to die. In about a week, the liver-soul is gradually diffused back into Nature as a life force. Immediately after death, before a significant amount of the liver-soul has diffused away, the liver-soul is sought by witches to extend their lives. Although its loss to witches does no harm to the first soul or to the living community, it is viewed as a desecration of the corpse, so a wake is held to prevent intrusion by witches. Knowing that the death will attract witches, a conjuror may use the wake to attempt to kill a witch, thus eliminating an enemy of the community. While a person is alive, his or her spiritual and physical strength are deterrents to witch attacks. Other deterrents, before and after death, are the strength and magical power of the fire on the household hearth, and the magical power, vigilance and knowledge of the conjuror.

The third soul is the soul of circulation. This soul is possessed by all animals, is a substance, has no individuality and is quantitative; there being more or less of it in the person or animal. This soul is located in the heart, and it creates blood. The living may be attacked, by a conjuror's magic, through the blood-soul by methods called "blood sucking" which produces anemic diseases.

After death, this soul takes a month to die, gradually diffusing back into Nature as a life force. It is of no use to witches or conjurors.

The fourth soul is the soul of energy, and is located in the bones. This soul is possessed by all animals, birds and fish that have bones. The bone-soul does not create physical substances, but creates spiritual energy which can be used by the conjuror to promote healing, treat illness that reduces energy, and as an aphrodisiac. In many Native American cultures and other cultures around the world, a powder of bone, horn or antler is used for medicinal purposes or as an aphrodisiac.

After death, this soul takes a year to die, gradually diffusing back into Nature, contributing its energy to the growth of crystals in the ground, especially to quartz crystals which are used in divination and conjuring. While this energy is diffusing from the corpse, and before it becomes concentrated in crystals, it is of no use to witches or conjurors.

The grave should be tended and kept free of weeds for a year after the person's death. After that, it is no longer tended because all the four souls have departed, and there is nothing of significance left in the grave. At that time, all mourning ends.

Conjurors and witches vary greatly in their power. Ordinary witches are solitary, secretive and use their magical powers selfishly only to extend their lives and health by stealing liver-soul from others. Among the ordinary witches, a few become conjurers of great knowledge and moderate magical power, sometimes called "white witches", and rise above the ordinary witches to unselfishly aid members of their clan or tribe. They will not admit to consuming liver-soul.

A few, rare individuals become great conjurors or Adawehi with great knowledge and vast magical power. They are the great "Raven Mockers" who assault the liver-souls of other tribes and of great rival conjurors like magical warriors. The last such conjuror, among the Cherokees, was Usawi (Oo-sah-wee) who lived more than 150 years ago.

CHAPTER 16
THE WAKE

Most of the lessons that Kawaya taught me were pleasant, but a few were not. One still frightens me when I think about it.

During the autumn of the year I was thirteen years old, an elderly Cherokee man, John Buckhorn, who lived near our farm and often told me stories about the old days , became ill and died. His family immediately sent for Kawaya to come to the Buckhorn home and be present at his wake. The family suspected that a witch had caused the illness and death of Mr. Buckhorn, and they believed the witch might attempt to violate his body during the night.

I happened to be at Kawaya's cabin when the boy arrived with the news of the death and to request that Kawaya come to the home of the dead man. I was shocked and saddened by the news that my friend had died, and I asked Kawaya if I could attend the wake. He said it would be all right if my parents would allow me. I immediately rode my little mare to my home, gave my parents the news of Mr. Buckhorn's death, and, after I finished my chores, received permission to attend the wake. My parents said they would be coming later, but said I could go immediately if I wished.

I arrived at the Buckhorn house a little before dark, and found that Kawaya and several family members and neighbors had already gathered. Kawaya had kindled a sacred fire in the fireplace and placed cedar and other herbs around the body and feathers around the doors. Some of the people were singing hymns while others were visiting or eating. Most of them had brought cooked food which was placed on the table in the front room or on the wood cookstove in the back room so that anyone who was hungry could help themselves. My parents arrived about an hour later. My mother brought a pie, still warm from the oven. They paid their respects and prepared to leave for home. I asked them if I could stay all night at the wake. At first, my mother was apprehensive about my staying all night, but Kawaya assured her he would watch after me, so, she let me stay.

The corpse was laid out on the bed in the front room, and Mrs. Buckhorn sat in her rocking chair near the bed. The fire burning in the fireplace provided some warmth against the chill of the autumn evening.   The fire and a kerosene lamp provided the only light in the room. Many of the people just came in with their food, placed it on the table or stove, viewed the body and paid their respects to Mrs. Buckhorn. Then, some got a plate of food and went outside on the porch or in the yard to visit awhile with neighbors before they left for their homes. Only a dozen or so people, including Kawaya and myself, would spend the entire night in the house with the corpse.

Kawaya was not related to the Buckhorns, nor was he a close friend. But he had been called to use his spiritual powers to protect the corpse from possible violation by a witch. I was merely there to pay my respects to my friends, the Buckhorns. I was not aware that I would play a role in the events that would happen during the night, but I believe that Kawaya knew that I would be tested.

I was hungry, having left home without eating supper, and it was not difficult for Mrs. Buckhorn to talk me into a couple of plates of food, topped off with a piece of my mother's apple pie. After I ate, I sat down on a folded quilt that Mrs. Buckhorn placed on the floor near the fireplace. I was determined to stay awake all night with Kawaya and the others. I listened to the singing for awhile, but, with my full stomach and the warmth from the fire, I soon fell asleep.

I awoke suddenly during the night and I sat bolt upright on the quilt. The room was silent except for the sounds of the fire and the soft snores in the room. Kawaya and the others were asleep in chairs or on pallets on the floor. I was evidently the only one awake in the room, and I wondered what had startled me from my sleep. I was about to lie back down when I saw, near the door, a sight that filled me with horror and turned my blood to ice water. It was an owl, perched on the back of a chair, its eyes glowing red in the dim light! I knew it was a witch, because they often take the form of an owl. It had come to do its gruesome work, and I was the only one awake!

The owl quickly took wing, in total silence, toward the bed upon which the corpse lay. I tried to cry out, to wake Kawaya and the others, but I could not make a sound. It was as if the owl's eyes had paralyzed me. As the owl landed on the body and turned its eyes away from me, I somehow gained control of my hands. I grabbed the small ash shovel that leaned against the fireplace, scooped into the hot coals of the sacred fire, and threw them at the owl. My aim was good; the coals hit the owl, whisps of smoke spurted out from the places where the glowing coals stuck to its feathers, and the owl flared up from the corpse.

Then, the owl again turned its glowing eyes to me, and flew directly for me! It landed on my head, grabbed its talons into my hair and began pulling out hair with its beak, like it was scalping me! I was again paralyzed and unable to speak or move. Suddenly, I felt the owl release its grip on my head, and as I looked up, I saw that a great eagle had locked its talons into the owl and a fierce fight was in progress above my head. There was a great beating of wings and feathers falling all around. I clearly saw the white head of the eagle, and it reminded me of Kawaya's white hair. As they fought, they rose higher, passing through the ceiling of the room, and I could see them no more.

I guess I passed out from fright, and I did not wake up until daybreak. Mrs. Buckhorn had built a fire in the cookstove and was making coffee. Some of the others in the room were stirring. I wondered if what had happened during the night had just been a dream. The more I thought about it, the more convinced I became that it had been a dream.

Meanwhile, one of the men in the room got up from his pallet and went outside to relieve himself. He quickly came back through the door, and without disturbing the others in the room, came over to Kawaya, who sat warming himself before the fire. The man whispered something to Kawaya, who rose from his chair and followed the man out through the door. I wondered what was going on, so I slipped over to the window to see.

There, face down on the ground in the front yard, lay a man named Patchett. He was a friend to no one, certainly not the Buckhorns, who had had trouble with him over the years. Some people said he was a witch. One of the men attempted to turn him over, but he was obviously dead and stiff as a board, his body coated with frost. Then I noticed several dark spots on his clothes, like they had been burned in several places.

Kawaya and the man came back into the house and got another man, and the three of them went back outside. I looked through the window again and saw the two men carrying the body, and following Kawaya into the woods. No one else in the house saw what happened.

I suddenly felt very tired and, since almost everyone in the room was still asleep, I laid back down on my pallet and quickly fell asleep. Later, when I awoke, I again wondered if it all had been a dream.

Then, nearby, I saw Mrs. Buckhorn with her broom sweeping up some feathers from the floor. I heard her say, to herself, that a pillow or the feather bed must have come unsown during the night, and she would need to sew it up again.

Afterwards, I never heard a word spoken about the incident, and I never spoke of it myself.

CHAPTER 17
KAWAYA'S DREAM

I heard my parents say that no one knew how old Kawaya was but he had to be in his eighties or nineties. He was a mystery to the local people, having moved, a few months before, into an abandoned cabin back in the woods up Barren Fork Creek where he lived by himself. No one knew where he came from, and when asked, he would only say he came from a far off place. Some guessed he might have come from the Cherokee Reservation in North Carolina, or from the Cherokees that went into Texas or Mexico.

I told you how he removed the warts from my hands with grains of corn. After that, we became friends and fishing companions. I called him Edudu (Aye-doo-doo; Grandfather) and he called me Saloli (Sah-low-lee; Squirrel).

I visited him often, two or three times a month; riding my horse to his cabin, and about once a month he visited my parents and me on our farm. Kawaya always walked the distance between his cabin and our farm, which was about five miles. Once I asked him if he didn't get tired on the walk from his house to ours, and he said no, when he got tired walking, he flew!

He loved to tell stories, and I loved to hear them. They were wonderful stories that stretched the horizons of my imagination. Some stories came from his dreams, and some came from the time when he was a boy. I figured he made up some of them because they were too strange to be true. For instance, he told about hunting buffalo when he was a youth; riding among the stampeding buffalo on his horse, and shooting them with arrows. I had read about the Plains Indians hunting buffalo like that, but I knew the Cherokees had never hunted buffalo from horseback[16].

The strangest story he ever told me was about his death. He said he lived in a far away place and his name was Black Elk. He grew old and one night he died. He said he looked down on his body as he went out through the smoke hole in the top of his tipi. He flew through the sky to the great star path, and began his walk south toward the center. He was nearly to the center, where the Great Spirit lives, when he met an old woman standing in the path.

"Why do you block my path, Grandmother?" he asked. "I have walked the Spirit Path through my life and now I come home."

"None who have come here have earned more honor than you," the old woman said, "and you may pass if you wish. But I was sent to ask you to return to earth to do another task."

So Kawaya returned to earth, to this place where he now lived. I told him I was glad he came back, and I think he was also glad, because we had many good times together. He didn't tell me what task the old woman had given him to do. Evidently, it wasn't too urgent, because he always had time for us to gather roots, nuts, berries, and herbs from the woods, to find wild bee trees, to catch fish from the streams, and to tell each other about our dreams.

---

[16] After reaching adulthood, I learned that the Cherokees did hunt buffalo after the removal to Indian Territory in 1839. The buffalo herds were not killed off until the 1870s. So, Kawaya could have hunted buffalo from horseback.

CHAPTER 18
KAWAYA'S CABIN

Kawaya lived by himself in a cabin a few miles up Barren Fork Creek from the farm where my parents and I lived. When my mother saw his cabin for the first time, she didn't say anything until we got home where she pronounced him "shiftless". But to me, Kawaya's cabin was a wonder and I loved to spend time there. If someone had deliberately set out to design a place where a boy could feel comfortable, they could not have built a better place.

The main room was built of logs and roofed with hand-split shingles. There was a shed room on the back built of gray, sawmill oak boards and bats, and it had a tin roof. There was porch across the front of the cabin, roofed with shingles like the main cabin. The main room. was about twelve feet square and had a fireplace on one side wall. The shed room was the kitchen, and had a wood-burning cookstove with a stovepipe that went up through the tin roof.

To me, the wonderful thing about the cabin was not its construction but the degree to which it had returned to nature. When I was in it, it somehow reminded me of being in a cave or a hollow tree. It was hard to determine where nature ended and the cabin began. In the summertime, as you approached the cabin, coming up the trail from the creek, you would not realize it was there until you were near the porch. There was no road, electric lines or anything else connecting it to the outside world.

The walls and part of the roof were covered with leafy Virginia creeper vines so that the cabin was nearly invisible among the trees and underbrush. Some of the vines did not stop at the walls. In several places, they had found small openings in the chinking between the logs where they grew through between the logs, up the inside walls and across the ceiling. At intervals, the vines put out shoots, searching for light, which hung down a foot or more from the ceiling. Kawaya kept the vines and leaves on the outside walls cut off the windows so that light and air could come in but otherwise, he left them grow where they pleased.

The creatures of the woods evidently considered the cabin as part of nature because they came and went as they pleased. The first time I visited Kawaya at his cabin, I was surprised when a fox squirrel hopped in through the open door and onto the table. Kawaya took a hickory nut from a basket beside the fireplace, and the squirrel took it from his fingers. Kawaya saw the surprised expression on my face and explained that, a couple of years earlier, he had found a nest with three baby squirrels in a hollow tree that a spring storm had uprooted. He raised the squirrels and returned them to the wild, but they returned for a visit from time to time. Then some wild squirrels followed their example and came in the house too. He said they didn't hurt anything and he enjoyed their company. Over the years, I saw many animals and birds that lived near or with Kawaya.

There were no screens on the windows and no screen door so, in the summertime when the doors and windows were open, the insects also came and went as they pleased. There were few mosquitoes; Kawaya kept gourds around to attract purple martins, and they kept the mosquitoes under control. Hornets kept the houseflies under control. Many times, while we were eating at the table, a pesky fly would buzz over the food only to be caught by a lightening quick hornet and carried away to its nest in the woods.

I got used to the mammals and birds, but the snakes sometimes gave me a start. When I spent the night with Kawaya, I slept on a pallet on the floor because he only had one small bed. One night, a black snake nearly scared me to death when it crawled across my leg. Kawaya said the snakes kept his cabin free of rats and mice. More than once, I saw Kawaya catch king snakes and carry them home where he turned them loose near his cabin. He said they killed poisonous snakes, and I never saw a poisonous snake around his place.

Kawaya had few possessions. As nearly as I can remember, the furnishings in his cabin consisted of a small wooden table and two chairs, a bed and a dilapidated wood cookstove, all of which the previous occupant had left in the cabin. He also had a kerosene lantern, a kerosene can, a fireplace poker, a cast iron stew pot, a wash tub, a coffee pot, a wash pan, two cast iron skillets, a water bucket, a gourd dipper, two blue metal cups, three blue metal plates, two forks, two spoons, a knife, several mason jars in which he kept honey, rice, beans, etc. and a large metal lard stand in which he kept bags of corn meal and flour.

Kawaya's cabin was different from the houses of most people; his cabin protected him from the rain and cold without isolating him from nature. When I was there, it felt more like a camp than a permanent house; as if nature could swallow it up at any time. Kawaya lived by the philosophy that man does not own the earth; he only camps for awhile and then moves on.

CHAPTER 19
HUNTING WILD BEE TREES

Kawaya made many of the things that he needed, and gathered or caught much of what he ate from the woods and streams so he needed little money. He said a man could be rich in either time or money, and he would rather be rich in time.

From the store, he got a few staples such as corn meal, coffee, salt, lard and salt pork. Instead of paying for those things with money, he usually traded with honey which he took from wild bee trees in the woods, and the storekeeper in turn sold the jars of honey. I spent many summer days hunting wild bee trees with Kawaya.

One method that we used to locate bee trees was to hunt for honey bees along a creek or at a spring or pond; looking for bees that were watering and then attempting to course them to their colony within a hollow tree. Bees have a favorite spot to water, usually at the nearest water to the bee tree.

91

The workers land at the edge of the water and spend a half-minute or more loading up with water. Then, heavily laden, they fly slowly up, circle to get their bearings, and then fly in a straight "beeline" to the hive tree.

Once we located a spot where bees were watering, we would watch to determine the direction they flew. Kawaya had the most remarkable ability to see the bees of any person I have ever known. Sometimes the bee course would cross a field before entering the woods and, if the sun was right, he could see the individual bees going through a particular opening in the leaf canopy a hundred yards away. We would pick out some distinguishing feature of the trees to mark the spot where we lost sight of the bees and then walk to that spot.

Then, we would watch the open area back toward the water and attempt to spot the bees flying from the water toward us, and then follow their course through the trees until we could no longer see them and mentally mark that spot. By continuing this process of observing their course a segment at a time, and if everything went well, we would eventually arrive at the bee tree; sometimes a half-mile or more from the water.

Of course, the process is much easier to describe than to actually do. To see a single honey bee, flying at high speed through the shadows and sunbeams of the leaf canopy fifty feet above you, is not an easy thing. Kawaya would spot the course and then go to great lengths to help me see it, pointing out the exact spot to watch for the next bee. Sometimes I could see it and sometimes I couldn't.

So, Kawaya made a bee box for me, and taught me our second method for locating a bee tree. The bee box was an ingenious little box with two compartments. It could be used on bees that were feeding on flowers. We would open the lid of the box and catch bees that were on flowers, and then open the partition to the other compartment that contained a piece of honeycomb. The bees would immediately begin feeding on the honey and we would open the lid and set the box on the ground in a clearing. Once loaded, the bees would fly back to the hive with news of their find and soon several bees would be working the box, allowing us to course them. Then we would close the lid, trapping some bees inside, move along the course a ways, open the lid and let the bees fly back to the hive with information about the new location. We would repeat the process until we eventually arrived at the bee tree.

We knew we were close to the bee tree when the lines of bees coming to and from the bee tree crossed. Once we arrived in the vicinity of the bee tree, it was often difficult to find which of several possible trees contained the bees, and where they were entering the tree. Here I was on an equal basis with Kawaya because, although he could see the bees better than I, my hearing was better than his. I would listen for the sound of the bees swarming around the hole that was the entrance to their colony within the hollow tree. I would often locate the entrance by sound before he could locate it by sight.

It was necessary to cut down the bee tree to get the honey it contained, but we actually cut few of the bee trees we found. We would usually find ten to twenty bee trees during a summer, but most of those we found for fun rather than cutting. A bee tree would yield thirty to a hundred pounds of honey, so a couple of trees usually provided all the honey Kawaya and my family needed for the year.

With a hatchet or knife, Kawaya would make three slash marks on the trunk of a tree he intended to cut and other bee hunters respected the mark and left the tree alone. He preferred to cut trees which contained colonies of the larger bees that were yellow with black stripes. They were gentler and easier to handle than the colonies of smaller, black bees which were very aggressive, and would fight when disturbed, and even chase you.

When the time was right, usually in late summer, we would return to the tree with the equipment we needed to cut the tree, a tub to hold the honey and an empty gum for the bees. We would cut down the tree with a crosscut saw and wait for the bees to settle down. We tied rags around the cuffs of our pants and coats, put nets over our hats and began cutting into the hollow that contained the bees, sawing across the grain above and below the hollow, and then splitting out pieces of the trunk with an axe. The bees would go crazy and we would use a bee smoker containing smoldering rags to calm the bees, but we still figured on getting some stings.

We would remove the honeycomb to the tub and then Kawaya would locate the queen in the brood chambers, gently pick her up while her attendants covered his hand, and shake her off in front of the empty bee gum we had brought. The queen would crawl into the gum, followed by her attendants and then the other bees would begin entering the gum. By dark, the entire colony would be in the gum. We would carry the tub of honey and our tools home and return next morning before daylight to get the bee gum. We would plug the entrance hole and carry the gum home. I took some of the hives home to our farm, and Kawaya gave others to other folks who wanted bee hives. It was necessary to feed the bees on sugar water over the first winter, but then the hive would provide the family with honey for years. Kawaya didn't keep any bee hives for himself; I guess he enjoyed hunting the wild ones too much.

CHAPTER 20
THE LITTLE PEOPLE

One summer evening when I was a small boy, I was walking along the dusty country road, near where the trail to Kawaya's cabin started, when I came across an unusual, weaving track in the dust. I had often seen tracks, made by snakes, which looked like this but this track was a foot wide! Being a boy with an active imagination, I immediately concluded it was the track of a huge snake. The track came down the road, went into the weeds beside the road and then into the woods. Although I had never seen such a snake, I had heard stories about them and once saw a picture in a magazine of one that had swallowed a goat.

I decided to run to Kawaya's cabin, which was about a mile down the trail, and get him to come and look at the track. I had run only a short distance when I met Kawaya coming up the trail. I thought it strange that he would be coming out to the road that late in the evening, but I quickly forgot that and told him about finding the big snake track. He smiled and said he was on his way to see it when we met. I wondered how he knew about the track but I didn't ask; I had learned long before that Kawaya often knew of things before they happened or that happened at a distance from him.

He smiled when he saw the track and suggested that we follow it. I told him it might be dangerous but he said that I should not worry, it was a safe thing to do. We followed the track from the road, through the weeds that were still mashed down from the weight of the monster, and into the woods. We had followed it through the woods for a half mile or more when darkness began to fall. I reminded Kawaya that perhaps we should be starting back but he said we were almost there, although I had no idea where "there" was. A moment later, he stopped, turned toward me and motioned for me to look ahead. In the dim light, I saw movement a short distance ahead and then made out the forms of three little men rolling a large watermelon along on the ground! I remember thinking that the watermelon was as tall as they were!

I started to say something, but Kawaya put his fingers up to his lips to indicate that I should remain silent. Soon the little men were out of hearing and Kawaya explained. The men were Yvwi Junasdi (Yuh-wee Joo-nah-sdee; Little People). For the past three nights, Kawaya had been coming to a clearing in the woods, near where we were, where the Little People were having a feast and dance. Each night, they brought in food, such as the watermelon the four little men were rolling, which they had taken from a farmers watermelon patch near the road.

I had heard my parents and others speak of the Little People as long as I could remember. Their mischief was responsible for many of the lost items and accidents around the farm. I had often heard my parents and others say, when something became lost, "The Little People took it." If the lost item was later found, they would say, "The Little People brought it back." Sometimes, during the night, we might hear the dishes rattle in the kitchen or anytime, day or night, a dish or some other object might mysteriously fall and break and these incidents were often blamed on the Little People.

Some of our neighbors feared the Little People. Some said the Little People would circle a house smoking their pipes and conjuring the people inside the house. Our family considered the Little People mischievous but not evil or harmful. We knew the Little People considered it their right to help themselves to whatever they needed, but they only took food or other things from people who had more than they needed

Getting back to my story, the woods were now quite dark, although the full moon was rising which, with the stars, produced enough light for walking. We continued in the direction where Kawaya knew the clearing was located. When we arrived near the clearing, I could faintly see movement ahead. Kawaya gave me a plant he had with him and told me to rub it on my eyes. After using the plant, I found I could see a large number of Little People, perhaps a hundred, and the clearing, almost as clearly as daylight.

Kawaya told me to wait there and he walked into the clearing. I expected the Little People to run away when they saw him, since he had previously been so careful not to be seen. But they recognized him and moved toward him; it was me that he hadn't wanted them to see. He talked to their Chief and Elders who turned their eyes in my direction, and then he walked back to me.

He asked me if I wanted to join in their feast and dance. He told me that, if I did, I must expect that they would play tricks on me because they were a mischievous people. Also, I must not tell anyone about my experience because people would think I was crazy. The reason I am telling you this story now is that I have reached the point where I no longer care if people think I am crazy. I told Kawaya yes, I would like to join them.

They welcomed me but I couldn't understand what they were saying; their language sounded like mice squeaking. Kawaya gave me another plant and told me to rub it on my ears and then I was able to understand their language.

Some of the Little People escorted me to the dance area near the center of the clearing and offered me a seat on a mat lying on the ground. When I sat down, I discovered, to my surprise, that they had placed the mat over a shallow hole in the ground, and when I sat down, I fell backward into the hole. Everyone laughed and I managed a half-hearted, embarrassed laugh. That was the first of many tricks that were played on me that night.

As the Little People prepared for their feast, many animals came from the woods to the edge of the clearing to watch the festivities, and the trees surrounding the clearing were filled with owls, herons, whip-poor-wills and other night birds. The dark woods were illuminated by light from the rising full moon, the stars, hundreds of fireflies that twinkled in the trees and the eerie phosphorescent glow of foxfire on the logs.

I finally found a safe seat on a glowing log as the feast began. Besides the watermelons, one of which I had mistaken for a snake (There was a good laugh all around when Kawaya told them about that) there were many other fruits, nuts, berries, fresh vegetables, hen's eggs, bread, rolls, pies, cakes, fruit jars filled with pickles, canned fruit and vegetables and all sorts of other good things to eat. All of the food had been gathered from the woods, farms, cellars or houses in the area. The Little People cooked nothing themselves and, evidently, they did not use fire. Kawaya told me they did not kill animals or eat meat.

The feast, along with much frolicking and playing of tricks, lasted for perhaps two hours. After the feast, the people assembled for the dancing and singing. The Little People gathered in groups around the dance circle according to their clans. The Cherokees have seven clans, the Little People have thirteen clans.

The Headman or Headwoman from each clan stood in front of their group, holding a lolo (low-low; cicada). They would stroke the cicada and it would begin its strange, buzzing chant. The other clan members then moved into the circle and began a joyful dance to that strange chant. Outside the circle, I could see the tiny children, mounted on rabbits and holding on to the rabbits' ears, laughing and squealing as the rabbits leaped and danced beneath the moon.

I mostly sat and watched, although I once briefly joined the dancing when someone dropped a large spider down the back of my shirt.

Sometime during the night I fell asleep and I awakened the next morning on my pallet in Kawaya's cabin. He said the Little People carried me there to repay me for all their tricks I had endured with good nature.

Since that night, whenever I see a watermelon, I call it Utana Inada (oo-tah-nah ee-nah-dah; big snake) and chuckle to myself.

CHAPTER 21
KAWAYA'S REVENGE

Some said Kawaya was a Medicine Man and had special powers. I believe he did have special powers because I witnessed several things that defied explanation. I believe his special powers came from his great wisdom and his special relationship to Nature and the Eternal One. He walked the Spirit Path and, in return, I believe Nature and the spirits protected and nurtured him. During the years I knew Kawaya, I saw many examples of this protection and nurturing, which some might call luck or coincidence, but which occurred with a dependable regularity that went far beyond mere luck or coincidence.

The story I will tell you illustrates the power of Kawaya's special relationship to Nature and the spirits. I hesitate to tell this story because, even after all these years, it is still painful for me to remember. But it contains lessons which should be remembered.

Kawaya was a gentle man who lived in harmony with nature. He had a deep reverence for life and I never saw him deliberately harm any living thing; human, plant or animal, except in self defense or to obtain food and the other things necessary to sustain his life. For example, during the summer months, wasps would build large nests under the roof of his porch directly over his cabin door. Most people would have killed the wasps and knocked down the nests, fearing that the wasps would sting them. Kawaya let them build and stay year after year, and they never bothered him.

His gentle nature was one reason I had so much difficulty dealing with his trouble with a couple of young thugs, brothers, that lived in our community. I will call the brothers "Smith", not using their real name to protect the other members of their family, most of whom were good people. I knew the brothers from the school we attended although they were several years older than I. They were constant trouble-makers at school and in the community.

Our school had two rooms: the "little" room contained grades one through four and the "big" room contained grades five through eight. The teachers in the school were a pretty young woman, Miss Ross, and a nervous little man with glasses, Mr. Duncan. The Smith brothers delighted in making up filthy jokes about them.

The Smith brothers made life miserable for Miss Ross in the little room and then, when they were both nearly grown, they finally "graduated" to the big room and made life miserable for Mr. Duncan. Finally, one day they beat up Mr. Duncan at school and they didn't come to school any more after that.

Their behavior worsened as they reached adulthood and spent a large part of their time drunk on moonshine whiskey. They often rode through the community on their horses firing pistols into the air and scaring people half to death. They got into fights at several dances and pie suppers and had several brushes with the law.

One day in August, I rode my horse up Barren Fork Creek to Kawaya's cabin and found him repairing the porch roof of his cabin which, in front, had fallen down almost to the floor. I knew we hadn't had a storm and I couldn't imagine what could have happened.

He told me what happened while I helped him replace the posts that held up the porch roof. The Smith boys had ridden up to his cabin, drunk, and yelled for him to come outside. Kawaya was already outside, in the woods nearby, and he decided to remain hidden and watch.

When Kawaya didn't come out of the cabin, the Smith boys got off their horses and tied them to the porch posts. They stepped up onto the porch and pounded on the door, which wasn't locked, and demanded money to buy more moonshine. Then, one brother pulled a pistol from his pocket and fired it in the air and all hell broke loose. The shot spooked the horses which shied backward, jerking down the porch posts which let the roof fall on the brothers' heads, knocking them to the floor. But, that was minor compared to the fact that wasps had built two large nests, each as big around as a man's hat, under the porch roof and the swarm of angry wasps began stinging the brothers and their horses. The squealing, bucking horses tore down the hollow toward Barren Fork Creek followed by the brothers, yelling, waving their arms, and surrounded by a cloud of wasps!

Some of their folks went looking for them the following morning when the brothers' horses came home without them. They finally found the brothers wandering in the woods unable to see because their eyes were swollen shut.

A couple of weeks later, the brothers, on horseback, came upon Kawaya walking home from the store. They roped and dragged him and left him unconscious in the woods, not knowing if he were alive or dead. He later managed to get to his cabin where I found him the next morning. He was in his bed, bruised and cut and unable to get out of bed.

I rode, as fast as I could, home and told my parents what had happened. My mother wanted to send to Tahlequah for the Doctor, but my father knew that Kawaya would not use the white man's medicine. They saddled their horses and rode back to Kawaya's cabin with me. They determined that no bones were broken and he told them how to prepare some poultices from moss and plants that grew along the spring branch and medicinal teas from plants he kept dried in his cabin.

The next morning, my mother and I rode home to take care of our livestock. My father stayed with Kawaya for several days until he could care for himself. My father thought it better that he stay in case the Smith boys came again. I had never seen my father so angry. He had brought his rifle and I believe he hoped they would come back.

I rode each day to check on Kawaya and my father and take in food and other things they needed. We notified the sheriff who came out and talked to the Smith boys but he said there was nothing he could do since there were no witnesses and the Smith boys denied the whole thing. My father was angered by the "do nothing" sheriff who made no attempt to control the making of illegal moonshine and the misery it brought. I think that was when my father decided to run for sheriff himself and, later, he ran and was elected.

The day my father rode home from Kawaya's cabin, I stayed with Kawaya and we had a chance to talk alone for the first time. I was outraged that justice had not been done and my hatred for the Smith boys had grown as each day passed. I found myself constantly planning ways do them serious harm. I told Kawaya I could easily ambush and shoot them both with arrows before they could get off a shot with their pistols.

He said, "Saloli, you are mistaken to think that justice will not be served. Every wrong is punished just as every good is rewarded. The spirits and

Nature always maintain a perfect balance and see that every debt is paid."

I said, "I have heard the preacher in church talk about hell, but that is too long to wait for the Smith boys to get what is coming to them!"

He answered, "I am not speaking about the hereafter, sometime in the future, but the earth here and now. You need never worry; whatever reward is called for, it will come without fail. Do not do anything foolish; let the spirits take care of it."

I believed him but I still wasn't satisfied. However, my anger cooled as the days passed, school started and fall approached. The Smith boys kept a low profile for awhile and life was peaceful again. Then, one morning, someone brought the electrifying news to school--the Smith boys were dead!

The county newspaper carried the details the following day. The Smith boys were driving their car at night, at high speed, on the highway near Tahlequah. Their car left the highway and ran into the front of a store building. The car was wedged between the side of the building and the metal posts that held up an awning on the store so that the car doors could not be opened. Witnesses said the brothers did not appear to be hurt and they were laughing and passing a mason-jar of moonshine when the car caught fire. It was impossible to get them out of the car as the flames engulfed it.

The newspaper also stated that witnesses claimed to have seen a third person, an old man, sitting in the back seat but, evidently, they were mistaken because only two bodies were recovered.

Justice is always served, although, for most people, not as quickly or dramatically as for Kawaya. As I said, Kawaya had a special relationship with the spirits and Nature. The spirits and Nature rush to aid those who walk the Spirit Path.

CHAPTER 22
WHOOPING

When I was a boy growing up in the hills of the Cherokee Nation in Northeastern Oklahoma, people used to whoop a lot. I don't know why; maybe they were venting their frustrations or anger or happiness or maybe it was because they were bored and had nothing better to do. Anyway, they whooped a lot. I don't know if I inherited the tendency to whoop or learned it, but it is a trait I carry to this day. I often have trouble controlling it and sometimes it gets me into trouble, as I will tell you shortly.

Perhaps I should define the whoop so you can better understand my story. My dictionary defines "whoop" as "a loud yell expressive of eagerness, exuberance, or jubilation." That is a satisfactory beginning of a definition but tells us nothing of the qualities of a proper whoop, its effect on a listener or, as you will soon see, the problems it can cause.

The proper whoop has certain, well defined limits of length, volume and pitch. The whooper sort of says the word "whoop", only extended like "whoooop" to last for one or two seconds. The volume is loud--the louder the better--and an excellent whoop will carry for miles through the hills on an autumn evening. The pitch begins fairly high and rises through the whoop to suddenly end with the lips together to form the letter 'P" at the end.

Before Columbus, the Cherokees' favorite pastime was making war, and whooping was an integral part of warfare, so the whoop was developed to an art form. The war-whoop was designed to encourage the whooper and terrify the whoopee.

My father lived, of course, long after the glory days of the pre-Columbian Cherokees, but he still loved to whoop. He had a magnificent whoop, high pitched and yet manly with just the right pitch and great volume that could carry for miles. Sometimes we would be out in the woods on a fine spring or autumn day hunting and he would suddenly, without warning, let go with a whoop that would make the hills and hollows ring and scare me half to death! I think that, sometimes, he would just get to feeling so full of joy that he had to whoop to keep from bursting. Sometimes, from far off in the woods, a kindred spirit would return his whoop, almost like an echo.

I worked on my own whoop, but I couldn't get a manly pitch and volume at the same time. If I tried to get more volume, it came out too high pitched and I sounded like a girl in distress. That was embarrassing, especially if someone heard me and ran to the rescue.

The quality of my whoop improved with age but I still had trouble controlling my urge to whoop. Frankie, my girlfriend who would later become my wife, took over my education concerning whooping; that is, when it is proper to whoop and when it is not. Whooping is always appropriate at rodeos and baseball games, sometimes appropriate at other events, but is never appropriate at weddings, funerals and church. I have had no success convincing her that an occasional whoop livens up these latter festivities. So, I try to restrain myself and she will tell you herself that I have made some progress in all these areas.

Actually, it hasn't been too hard for me to suppress the urge to whoop at weddings and funerals because I usually can't find much to whoop about at either one. We are still working on church. Frankie is a Church Elder and she informs me that she has carefully searched the rules and found no instance where whooping is a prescribed part of any services in the Presbyterian Church. But like I said before, she says I am improving and, now-a-days, she often lets me go to church without duct tape over my mouth.

I have presented all the preceding information to help explain to the world and especially to Dave Cloud why I whooped in his secret fishing hole.

It happened this past June near Homer, Alaska. My friend, Dave Cloud, who lives in Homer, took me in his boat across Kachemak Bay to a secret spot he discovered where the King Salmon return in great numbers during a brief period each year. It is a beautiful hidden fjord beneath the snow capped peaks and glaciers. Down in the clear, cold water, I could see the giant King Salmon swimming by the tens and scores and hundreds. It was the most beautiful, tranquil, unspoiled place I had ever seen and it was all ours; there was not another boat in sight!

We rigged our fly rods, because any less elegant equipment would have profaned this place and these fish. I cast and immediately saw a giant King rise toward the end of my line. I set the hook, half in hope and half in fear, and found myself fast to that great, beautiful, leaping fish that took my breath with my line. He should have escaped a dozen times but luck was with me that day and, after thirty minutes

109

of the most exciting battle of my life, Dave netted him and I whooped!

It was probably my best whoop ever; there were stories later that it was heard 200 miles away in Anchorage, but that was probably an exaggeration. Anyway, before we got the fish on the rope stringer, the first boat showed up. Within thirty minutes, we were surrounded by boats so that we had no place to cast. Finally, Dave shook his head in disgust, started his outboard and moved out from the crowd and we met more boats coming.

Thankfully, Dave is a forgiving soul and I didn't have to swim back across Kachemak Bay. I promised that if he would take me fishing again I would not whoop. That, and a case of beer, brought him around. He took me to another spot a few days later and I caught another King. Luckily, it was a smaller fish, only twenty pounds, and I controlled my urge to whoop. He even invited me to fish with him again next year, but I'm taking no chances; I'm packing duct tape in my tackle box.

CHAPTER 23
SLOW

All my life, I have been slow. As a child, I was a slow learner. It wasn't that learning was difficult for me, it just took more time for me than it did for others.

I remember, in the fifth or sixth grade, our teacher used to have dictionary drills. He passed out dictionaries to everyone in the class. Then, he would give us a word and everyone looked up the word as quickly as they could and raised their hand when they found it. I was usually the last one to find the word. Although I have never, in my life since that time, had the need to see how quickly I could look up a word, that experience, in his class marked me mentally and, I'm sure, in my permanent school records. In my mind, I saw myself as inferior to my classmates.

In high school, I took a typing class. The girls who sat on each side of me could type so fast I imagined that smoke came out of their typewriters. I, on the other hand, by the end of the year, had achieved the blinding speed of 36 words per minute. I hated every minute of the class, because I felt inferior every day. But, for years now, I have made my living as a writer, typing at my word processor almost every day, and my lack of speed has never been a factor in my success or failure.

When we were given standardized tests to measure everything from achievement to IQ, I could never finish the test in the time allowed. I would have nearly perfect scores on the portion that I finished but, of course, my overall scores would be less than perfect. Once, when the results of a standardized test came back, my teacher called me up and showed me that I had made a perfect score on the part of the test I had finished, but, I had not gotten to the last quarter of the test. He told me that, if I were ever going to amount to anything, I was going to have to work faster, which for me was impossible. It seemed that my teachers were not really interested in how much I knew or my ability to reason, but whether I could mark the test quickly.

After high school, I spent many years in colleges and universities proving to myself and others that I was not inferior. I now have BS, MS, and Ph.D. degrees hanging on my wall that tell everyone that I am not inferior. But my old mental ghosts of inferiority have not been easily put to rest.

Through my life, I have come to realize that my slowness has been more of a blessing than a handicap. God is slow, like me. God is above time; a thousand years and a second are the same to God. My slowness has given me patience; patience to wait for God to show me the way that I should go.

CHAPTER 24
LOGIC VS. INTUITION

Soon after Frankie and I were married, I discovered that our minds worked differently. I took pride in having a logical mind while Frankie usually disregarded logic, and relied on pure intuition. At first, I tried to change her thinking by showing her the superiority of logic over intuition. After all, I was a student of the sciences and felt that logic was the key to everything. Now, looking back over the years, I find that I am the one who has changed.

In the early 1960s, Frankie and I moved to Los Alamos, New Mexico where I took a position teaching chemistry in the high school and Frankie took a position teaching second grade. The greatest collection of top scientists in the world had been assembled at Los Alamos during WW II to develop the atomic bomb and many of those scientists and others were still living and working at the Los Alamos Scientific Laboratories when Frankie and I moved there. Many of the students we taught were the children of scientists, heard science every day of their lives, loved it and could not get enough of it! I had some students, whose parents were world renowned nuclear chemists, who knew more about some specialized areas of chemistry than I knew! Frankie and I both enjoyed our teaching and living in Los Alamos, but not for the same reasons. I found it a wonderful, challenging world in which science and logic pervaded every facet of my life—except Frankie. It all had no more effect on her than a single raindrop on a mountain.

In the late 1960's, Frankie and I and our four children moved to Ft. Lauderdale, Florida where I would attend Nova University and earn my Ph.D. For three years, science, logic and computers dominated my mind. Frankie taught in Eisenhower School, part of the Nova Schools Complex and one of the most innovative experimental schools in the nation where she earned a reputation as one of their top teachers. Did those years of immersion in that environment change her dominant thinking pattern from intuition to logic? Not in the slightest degree.

Upon hearing this evidence, some might call Frankie merely stubborn, but I had learned better. I am not a fast learner, but over the years I became aware of a strange phenomenon relating to my logic and Frankie's intuition. Sometimes, based on logic, my assessment of a situation was correct and sometimes incorrect, but Frankie's assessment of the same situation, based on intuition, was never wrong.

The "truths" of the scientific disciplines, such as chemistry and physics, are best perceived through logic and mathematics. For example, through mathematics, cosmologists prove that everything in the universe was once compressed into a single point, smaller than the period at the end of this sentence and that everything that exists today was born in the gigantic and continuing explosion of that point. Such a conclusion came not from the intuition, but from logic and mathematics. Over the history of science, such scientific "truths" have changed or evolved each time new observations no longer fit the old "truth."

At this point, I would like to introduce the concept of beauty into our discussion because, in my mind, truth and beauty are linked. Beauty is another thing that seems to evolve, like truth. It has been said that beauty is in the eye of the beholder and, with each new fashion season, the definition of what is beautiful changes a bit.

But, such tricks as evolving truth and beauty are from man, not from nature. Through my life, I have become convinced that there is absolute truth and beauty that do not change. I learned, from Frankie, that absolute truth and beauty are usually best perceived by the intuition rather than by logic. Further, this absolute truth and beauty can be perceived by any human being through his or her intuition. The beauty I see in the world is not inherent in the world, but in my eye under the guidance of my intuition. And other people look at the same scene and perceive the same beauty that I see. Through his or her intuition, each person has access to the stream of truth and beauty that flows through all life and being in the universe.

I have learned to trust my intuition. As a student and, later, as a teacher and, finally, as a writer, I used to try to memorize or record facts and experiences that I thought I would need later for an examination, a lesson I would teach, or something I would write. I sometimes agonized over the fact that I did not remember, as well as I should, the experiences of my childhood or the things that my Cherokee Elders told me. But I have learned that, while those things were happening, my intuition was selecting those things that I would need without any conscious effort on my part. Through some channel

115

which I did not know, every truth that I should know, every person that I should meet, every experience that I should have, all have come to me, and each in its proper time. This realization is one of the sources of my belief in God.

I have been told, in letters or conversation, by many of my readers that my writing seems to reflect their own thoughts and feelings. That is because they have perceived the same truth and beauty that I have perceived, and to which every person has an equal right of access. The spirits speak to every person through his or her intuition. I make no pretense that my writing reflects some truth or beauty that is hidden from others, I merely have a knack for putting my perceptions into words; I am a messenger. Others read my words and recognize their own perceptions and thoughts.

As I said in the beginning, my thinking has changed over the years. Now, I treasure both logic and intuition. Our clearest view of the world and of our own lives comes from the use of logic and intuition in combination.

I still have had no success in introducing logic into Frankie's thinking; she still operates totally on intuition. But recently, after years of totally avoiding the computer, she has started using it a little—to play solitaire and search the internet. Perhaps that is a first tiny crack in the dike, but I'm not betting on it.

CHAPTER 25
MRS. CRAVENS

Another of the special teachers who taught me to see was Mrs. Cravens. She taught me to see myself as worthwhile. Most teachers never realize the effect they have on their students' lives. Mrs. Dolly Cravens was my English teacher during my junior year in high school. She, and her class, had a great effect on my life.

For one thing, it was in her class that I first saw Frankie, the girl who would become my wife, the mother of our four children and my best friend. I sat at the back of Mrs. Craven's classroom and a pretty, dark-haired girl, who sat on the front row, kept turning and looking back at me, and she stole my heart. Frankie and I went together through our junior and senior years of high school and through four years of college before we married. Our marriage has prospered, happily, for forty-five years.

Mrs. Cravens' personal effect on me resulted from her recognition of me as an individual rather than merely another face in her class. I wrote a story which I called, "The Hunter," as an assignment in her class. When she returned the stories in class, she said she would like to talk to me for a minute after class. I figured I was in trouble, which was usually the case when a teacher asked to see me after class.

After class, she told me that my story was excellent; that she had read stories published in magazines that were not as good as mine. She said I had a "lucid" way of expressing myself.

I had no idea what "lucid" meant, so, as soon as she excused me, I headed for the library to look it up in the dictionary. Then, I couldn't remember whether the word she used was "lucid", meaning "suffused with light, clear to the understanding" or "lurid", which means "wan and ghastly pale in appearance, causing horror or revulsion." I was pretty sure she had said "lucid", but, whichever word it was, I took it as a compliment.

I wrote other stories which Mrs. Cravens praised and I developed a love for writing. But the thought of going into writing as a profession never occurred to me. In my mind, a poor Cherokee boy knew nothing or had no experiences that would be of interest to anyone. I would become a doctor or a lawyer, become rich and famous and drive back to my parents' house in a big, shiny car.

I enrolled in the college in Tahlequah and made good grades, but quickly learned I could never afford to go somewhere else to medical or law school. I could get a degree in chemistry from our local college so I studied chemistry. I earned a degree in chemistry, and then took a position as a chemist in industry. Later, I went into teaching, which I enjoyed, but my deep desire to be a writer always stayed with me.

118

When our children completed school and left home, I told Frankie I wanted to quit teaching and write. She told me to go for it. I have been writing now for about twenty years. Neither my teaching nor my writing has made me rich or famous, but there have been other rewards; both have allowed me to touch many lives. Presently, my writing brings me joy and fulfillment and, through my writing, I have played a small part in helping to preserve our Cherokee culture and have made many good friends.

Thank you, Mrs. Cravens, for your gift to me. I send you my love and my appreciation. I, and many others, owe so much to you.

CHAPTER 26
THE HERMIT

During the 1950's, in the summers, I would go float-fishing far up the Illinois River from my home near Tahlequah. My girl-friend who would later be my wife, Frankie, would take me, along with my boat, camping equipment and fishing gear by road almost to the Arkansas line; about sixty miles up the river. From that point, I would spend four or five days and nights alone on the river, floating and fishing by day and camping on the bank at night. The river was sparkling clear and danced like a living thing through the forested hills and bluffs of the Cherokee Nation. I loved the river and the solitude; usually I would see no one for days and never more than two or three people on the entire trip.

On this trip, I made camp the first evening under a rock overhang near the river, since it looked like rain, and I had no tent. I dropped my new Ray-O-Vac flashlight which hit a rock, denting the edge of the front and cracking the glass. Later, while baiting some limb-lines, I dropped the flashlight into the water. I could see the flashlight, still shining, lying on the gravel bottom in the deep water. I could have dived for it, but I decided the unlucky flashlight wasn't worth the trouble.

The next evening, I began looking for a good spot to camp for the night. As I came through a stretch of swift water and into a large deep hole of water, I noticed a boat tied back in a little slough where a spring branch ran into the river. I paddled downstream about half-way through the hole and pulled in on a gravel bar where I set up camp.

With my fly rod, I caught a few small green sunfish, that local people call "black perch" (in Cherokee, agola; pronounced ah-goe-lah), to use for bait on several limb-lines I had tied to willow branches hanging over the water. I hoped to catch some catfish (julisdanali; joo-lees-dah-nah-lee) during the night. Then I returned to camp, built a fire, fried some fish for my supper and ate as the fireflies filled the trees along the river, and the stars came out above me.

I had almost finished eating when I noticed a moving light up the river, evidently someone carrying a kerosene lantern, near where I had seen the boat tied. I could see someone get into the boat and then paddle downstream toward me. I figured it was someone coming to bait out a trotline, but the boat pulled up to the gravel bar near my camp and a man got out. He was a short, stout, old Cherokee man, dressed in tattered overalls. He wore very thick glasses; it looked like he was looking through the bottoms of two coke bottles, and he had a little hooked nose that looked like a beak. I thought to myself that he looked like an owl.

"Osiyo (oh-see-yoe; hello)," he greeted me. "Osiyo," I returned his greeting.

I asked him if he wanted some coffee (kawi; kah-hwee) and he said, "Howa (hoe-wah; Okay)," and he sat down on the gravel near my fire. I had only the one cup, that I had used for my coffee, so I rinsed it in the river and poured him some coffee. He tasted it and said, "Osda (oh-sdah; good), wado (wah-doe; thank you)". I still had two pieces of fried fish and offered them to him, but he declined, saying he had already eaten. He didn't seem ready to talk so I ate the fish, pulled some horsetail plants growing at the river's edge and scoured my skillet with them.

After a few minutes, he broke the silence by asking if I played checkers. I was a bit surprised, but I answered yes, I played a little. Actually, I considered myself quite an accomplished checker player but I always concealed that from a potential victim. I had learned to play checkers from some of the local masters at the country store near my boyhood home.

The old man asked me if I would like to play a game of checkers before I slept. I said I wouldn't mind. He suggested that I come in my boat to where he kept his boat and follow the trail to his cabin. Then he got back into his boat and paddled away.

Before I left camp, I unfolded a small Herter's candle lantern I always carried in my gear and lit it since there was no moon and I figured I would need a light. (You will remember I had lost my flashlight the night before.)

I found his little cabin a quarter mile up the hollow from the river. He was sitting outside, in front of the cabin, waiting for me. His lantern hung in a nearby tree and underneath was a little square table on which sat the remains of his supper. When we got ready to play checkers, he cleared off the table and I saw it had a faded checker board painted on top. He

123

produced a Prince Albert tobacco can which held the checkers and we prepared to do battle.

Our first game went well. He played pretty well and, out of respect for his age and the fact that I was his guest, I took it easy on him and he beat me by a little. I had no doubt I could beat him the next game; I had been nice but now it was time to get serious. We started another game and I couldn't believe what happened. My "victim" beat me so quickly and so badly I couldn't believe it! The third game, I took an even worse beating!

I saw a twinkle in his owl eyes and he smiled the gentle smile of an old man who knows he has just taught a young man a valuable lesson. Then he told me his story.

He was a world class checker champion. He showed me several copies of "Grit", a little newspaper that rural kids used to sell to earn spending money and prizes. A regular feature in Grit was called "It's Your Move", which showed a checker board with checkers in a certain arrangement. The object was to figure your next series of moves to win. The old man had once been a regular contributor to the feature.

He had served in the army in World War I and, while in the army, he was given the opportunity to play checkers against the best players in the different branches of the service, and he beat them all. His eyes and lungs had been injured when he was gassed in France, and he had returned to the hills of the Cherokee Nation. Now, he preferred to live away from people and only went out to the store for supplies two or three times a year. He spent most of his time fishing, gathering wild foods and studying his greatest love, checkers.

We talked far into the warm summer night while the chuck-will's-widow (sgwalegwala; sgwah-lay-gwah-lah) and the barred owl (uguku; oo-goo-koo) called in the woods around us. He showed me many

124

series of checker moves he had developed over the years and could show me every move of the games he had played against great players many years before.

Finally, I knew it was time to go, although, we didn't know what time it was, since neither of us had a watch. I lit the candle in my lantern and the old man was very fascinated by it. He went into his cabin and returned with a Ray-O-Vac flashlight. I did a double take when I saw it because it looked exactly like the one I had lost in deep water the previous night twelve or fifteen miles back up the river. It even had a dent in the edge of the front and the glass was cracked exactly like the one I had lost. I knew it couldn't be the same flashlight, but it was certainly an odd coincidence. Anyway, he asked if I would trade my candle lantern for the flashlight. I agreed to the trade and gave him two extra candies I had with me.

He told me to stop and see him again the next time I floated the river and we would play some more checkers. I told him I would stop again. The next morning, I broke camp and continued my trip down the river.

A few weeks later, I enrolled in college and the following years were busy ones for Frankie and me, filled with study, marriage, and starting our family and careers. Years went by before I floated the upper river again. When I stopped to see the old hermit, he was gone and his cabin was in ruin. In the cabin, I found the pieces of his little table with traces of the checkerboard still painted on the top. I camped for the night there in front of the cabin, listening to the night birds, and remembering the lesson in humility I once learned in that place.

The next morning, while I was breaking camp, a Cherokee man carrying a fishing pole came walking down the hollow toward the river. I asked him about the old man who used to live in the cabin. I said I didn't know his name, but he was living there a few years before when I stopped and played checkers with him.

The fisherman told me that no one had lived in the cabin in over forty years; not since World War I. A young married couple had built the cabin and lived there. Then the husband went to fight in the war and was killed in France. The wife left and never returned and the unoccupied cabin fell into ruin.

I described the old man and our checker game, and the fisherman told me that other people had seen an old man carrying a lantern along the river at night. He said the local people called the old man "Sgili" (Sgee-lee). His words sent a chill through me— "Sgili", in the Cherokee language, means great horned owl, and also means ghost!

CHAPTER 27
THE ORIGIN OF DISEASE AND MEDICINE

The people in our community said Kawaya was a Medicine Man, but he would not call himself a Medicine Man. He would only say he was Yvwi (Yuh-wee; Human Being). Medicine Men or Women were not self-appointed; they were recognized by the people. It would not have been proper for Kawaya to declare himself a Medicine Man.

Kawaya told me many stories that had been passed down from the Cherokees of long ago. I want to share, with you, the story about how disease began and how medicine came to the Cherokees.

In the days when the world was new, man, the animals and the plants were all the same. They all spoke to one another and lived together in mutual respect and peace, and they helped one another. But man multiplied until he covered the earth and began to crowd out the other animals and plants. He also invented bows and arrows, blowguns, knives, spears and hooks which he used to kill the other creatures without their permission, and he showed no respect for their rights.

You should understand that it was not man's killing of animals for his food that offended the animals. They understood that all animals, including man, must kill other animals or plants for food. But man was not respectful of his fellow creatures, killing without asking pardon, sometimes killing for pleasure rather than for food, and killing more animals than he needed to feed his family. In addition, as he walked, man was not careful where he stepped, and he sometimes squashed the smaller creatures under his feet. Because of his lack of respect, the animals decided they must take action against man.

The first group to meet in council were the bears. The bears had once been Cherokees, but they had left the People to live in the forest. The council was called by old Chief White Bear.

The bears talked about the violations by man and decided that they would make war on man. Someone had the idea that they should make bows and arrows to use against man, since this was the weapon man used against the bears.

They found a good piece of black locust wood and made it into a bow. Then, one bear gave up its life so its intestines could be made into a string for the bow. They also made arrows for the bow.

When the first bear attempted to shoot the bow, his long claws hung on the bowstring and spoiled the shot. So, they decided he would cut off his claws and try again. This time, the arrow went true to the mark.

When it was decided that all the bears must cut off their claws so they could shoot bows, Chief White Bear objected. He said that without their claws, the bears would not be able to climb trees and dig for food. The bears were better off with their teeth and claws as weapons; therefore, they would not be able to use the bow. So the council adjourned without a solution to their problems with man.

The next group to call a council were the deer, under their Chief, Little Deer. Someone proposed that any hunter that killed a deer would be stricken with rheumatism unless he (the hunter) should ask the pardon of the deer he killed. Everyone thought this was a good idea.

So, the deer sent word to man as to what a hunter must do when he was forced, by necessity, to kill a deer. The hunter must ask the pardon of the deer he kills. Little Deer, who is small, white, and moves as swiftly and invisibly as the wind, will come to the place where the deer is killed and ask the spirit of the slain deer if it heard the prayer from the hunter for pardon. If so, the Little Deer goes on his way without further action. But if the hunter does not ask for pardon, Little Deer will follow the drops of blood to the hunter's house and cripple him or her with rheumatism.

The next group to call a council were the fish and reptiles under Chief Rattlesnake. Their proposal was that they make man dream of rotting fish and snakes so that man would lose his appetite, become sick, and die.

The next group to call a council, under Chief Grubworm, were the insects, birds and small animals. Each council member, in turn, condemned man for his cruelty and lack of respect. Of all those present, only Ground-squirrel had a favorable word to say about man, because he (Ground-squirrel) is small and man seldom hurts him. The other creatures fell upon Ground-squirrel, and he bears the marks of their scratches upon his back to this day. Then, someone devised a disease with which to inflict man. Everyone thought this was a good idea so another animal devised another disease and soon the council was in a frenzy. So many diseases were devised that not one person of the human race would be able to survive.

When the plants, which were friendly toward man, heard what had been done by the animals, the plants decided to help man. Each plant, from the greatest trees to the lowly moss, declared that each would make a medicine to cure one of the diseases placed upon man by the animals. It was the role of the Medicine Man or Woman to discover which plant would cure each disease. The spirit of the plant tells the Medicine Person which disease it cures. Kawaya told me that sometimes, if he did not know which plant to use for a particular treatment, the butterflies or moths would show him the plant that he needed.

Some people, upon reading the material above, will declare that it is superstitious nonsense. Others might say that pre-Columbian Cherokee medicine was comparable to the medicine of the European invaders at that time. I want to give you some food for thought with the following questions:

Why were the pre-Columbian Native Americans so healthy, compared to the Europeans of that time or compared to the Native Americans of today? The Native Americans had no acquired immunity to the diseases brought by the Europeans because those diseases were unknown among the Native Americans. Could it be that the "superstitious nonsense" of the Native American Medicine People had eliminated those diseases from their population thousands of years before the Europeans came? Could it be that they knew secrets for good health that were forever lost as the pompous white man systematically wiped out the cultures of the Native Americans?

Today, many of the practices of the ancient Native American Medicine People are being re-discovered by modern medicine. We are all aware of the modern medicines that have been derived from natural sources. Plant scientists are combing rain forests, oceans and back yards every day, looking for plants that will yield new, disease-fighting drugs. Other experiments are discovering the healing power of the human spirit, love, and touch. We are also learning to tap our inner power to heal ourselves.

A very wise MD told me, one night a few years ago, as we sat by the fire of our hunting camp on the King Ranch in Texas, that his medical practice was 10% modern physician and 90% Medicine Man.

CHAPTER 28
THE SPIRIT OF THE HUNT

I have been a hunter since I was a young boy. I hunted because I enjoyed it and it helped to put food on our table. But, among the ancient Cherokees and other Native Americans, there was also a spiritual aspect to hunting that made hunting different from most modern-day hunting. Those differences relate to the mental attitude with which the hunter approaches the hunt, the goals of hunting and the beliefs concerning man's relationship to animals, plants and all of nature.

I have been privileged to learn from some excellent Cherokee hunters and also to learn from hunters from other tribes. Of those I have hunted with, I believe the ones who retain the most of their primitive hunting skills were the Inupiat Eskimos of Alaska. They are still subsistence hunters as they have been for thousands of years. Although they now use many of the tools of the modern hunter, such as rifles and snowmobiles, they still retain many aboriginal skills in hunting and survival which have been lost by most modern hunters. They also retain many of their traditional beliefs about hunting and animals.

Several beliefs about hunting that are still common among the Inupiat hunters are similar to the beliefs which were common among the ancient Cherokees. During the time I spent among the Inupiats, I recognized several similarities between their traditional beliefs and the traditional beliefs of the Cherokees.

The Goals of Hunting:
The Inupiat hunter and the Cherokee hunter sought the animal primarily for the food and raw materials it provided. I don't mean to imply that the primitive hunter didn't enjoy hunting. Hunting was the second favorite pastime of the pre-Columbian Cherokees, right after war. Among the Inupiats and the Cherokees, the successful hunter enjoyed status in the tribe. Hunting stories, songs, dances and rituals played an important role in the daily social life of the tribes.

Killing the Animal:
When the Inupiat hunter kills an animal, he believes the animal "gives" itself to him rather than his taking the animal by force. I constantly heard such statements as, "In 10 years, 14 bowheads (whales) gave themselves to our crew," or "The bowhead surfaced near us but it was not ready to give itself up. It made one last dive and we did not see it again."
This belief was also held by the Cherokees. Before embarking on a hunt, the Cherokee hunter asked the spirit of the animal for permission to take its life. Then, for example, if a hunter killed a deer, he was to immediately ask the spirit of the deer for forgiveness. If the hunter failed to do this, "Little Deer", the Spirit Deer, would follow the hunter back to his home and inflict him with rheumatism.

"Morality" of the Hunter:
Cherokee and Inupiat hunters held a common belief that the "morality" of the hunter had an effect on his success. The Cherokees believed that Nature and the spirits aided the hunter that was Yvwi. The following story from the Inupiats, concerning a man named Katauq, illustrates this belief.

Katauq was sitting in his igloo one day when those with him noticed that he moved not a muscle, though he continued to breath. They knew he had gone "traveling"; his spirit had left his body to go see how things were at some other place.

Katauq's spirit traveled to a great meeting of bowhead whales. They gave him a parka to wear (the Inupiat refer to the layer of blubber and meat on the whale as its "parka"). When he put on the parka, he became as one of them. Traveling with the whales as a whale, he learned their habits and their ways.

As spring approached, the whales informed him that they would be traveling along the coast near Point Hope where they would be met by whalers. He would notice that some of the whaler's umiaks (skin boats) would be nice and light in appearance and some would be dark and dirty.

If he wished to be caught by a whaler, then he should surface near one of the clean and light boats. These belonged to good people; respectful people. They shared their catch with the children who had no parents, with widows, and with the Elders. They were kind people with good hearts. Their ice cellars were clean; good places for a whale to have its parka of meat and muktuk (blubber) stored. The dark, dirty boats belonged to people who did not share their catch and who were lazy. No whale wanted to give itself to those boats.

However, Katauq knew that if he went to the village as a whale and gave himself to the whalers, his spirit could not return to his human body. It could put on another whale parka, but it could never again be human. He could, however, fly back to Point Hope as an eider duck; and his spirit could return to his human body. He decided to do that.

Afterward, he told the people about his time with the whales, and let them know how the whales felt, and how they respected respectful people.

The Cherokee held similar beliefs concerning the morality of the hunter. The hunter cleansed his body before the hunt by fasting the day before the hunt, drinking the "black drink" which cleansed his system, sweating in the sweat lodge and bathing in the stream. He cleansed his mind through ritual, prayer and meditation. After the hunt, the kill was shared with others, outside the family, who were in need.

I want to point out the importance of "respect" in the story of Katauq. We might have expected the storyteller to say the most important attribute of the hunter was knowledge of the ways of animals, skill in the use of weapons, or care in planning before the hunt. But, to the Inupiat hunter, the most important attribute is respect. Most modern hunters do not consider respect for their quarry as being important to their success in hunting. I feel we might be better hunters and would certainly be better human beings with fewer environmental problems if we shared the Inupiat belief in the importance of respect for nature.

Role of the Shaman:

As the story of Katauq illustrates, the Inupiats had Shamans who were able to communicate with animals and the Spirit World. Through magic, the Shaman could cure illness, divine the hidden, and control events.

The Shaman played an important role in preparations for the hunt. He prepared potions, conducted ceremonies, and helped the hunters contact the spirits of the animals they sought. He interpreted the dreams and visions of the hunters and other signs in nature which related to the hunt and its outcome.

Shamans or Medicine Men were common among most of the tribes of Native Americans. Among the Cherokee, the conjurers or Adawehis

134

wore animal or bird masks and by signs, portents and ancient formulas directed the preparations for hunting or war. Unlike most tribes, the Cherokee gave status approaching that of the Adawehis to certain women who won honors in war. They were called "Pretty Women" and custom dictated that an assemblage of these women be present at every war council. They also gave advice concerning plans for group hunting and other aspects of tribal life.

Entrance of the Animal Spirit into Another Body:
After butchering the whale, the Inupiat hunters return the skull to the sea. As it slowly sinks, the hunters shout out in the voices of sea mammals, which they mix with calls of "Come back! Come back!" The skull will provide food for the creatures living below and tiny chunks of blubber are thrown to the sea gulls as their share. By doing these things, the hunters have shown proper respect and hopefully, the whale's skull will now put on another parka and return to the village in another season.

I know of no exact parallel among the Cherokee, in which the spirit of the slain animal was thought to put on a new body and return, perhaps to give itself again. However, the Cherokee believe the spirit lives on after the animal is killed, and that an animal spirit could change to another animal or even a human. Many of the Cherokee tales of witches involve such transformations. There is a parallel to the Inupiat custom of sacrificing part of the kill back to nature. At a feast after a successful hunt, the Cherokee customarily spit out, onto the ground, the first bite of food he or she takes as a token of returning part of what nature has given.

CHAPTER 29
CATCHING PIGEONS

Wild Passenger Pigeons (Ectopistes migratorius) were a major source of food for the pre-Columbian Cherokees living in what is now the southeastern United States. The vast flocks, sometimes numbering billions of birds, fed in the almost unbroken forests on beechnuts, acorns, and other tree seeds, fruits and berries, insects and other available foods.

Come with me now on an imaginary journey back to the olden days in the Cherokee Nation. We will spend a day learning how to hunt for woyi (woe-yee; pigeons) with a man named Woyi who received his name because of his great knowledge of these birds and his skill in harvesting them. Each year, he supplies the families of his town with thousands of pigeons for food.

We arrive at Woyi's house two hours before dawn. We are hungry but no food is offered; it is customary for hunters to fast before the hunt. We help carry his equipment, which includes several cane and wooden poles with cords attached to them, two woven split-cane bird cages, each containing a live pigeon, two net bags, and a leather pack with carrying straps. We leave his house in the darkness beneath a canopy of brilliant stars. Our eyes soon adjust to the darkness so that we can follow Woyi through the town and out through the guarded gate in the palisade of logs that surround the town. An owl is hooting from the woods down by the river.

We follow the trail through the cornfields and then into the trees that border the river, and then head through the woods parallel to the river. The trail is harder to see now in the deeper darkness of the woods, and I hold my free arm and hand in front of my face to protect it from the tree limbs that sometimes snap back from Woyi's passing.

Finally, we leave the river and follow a small spring branch that flows from the nearby hills. We are walking through a forest of tall trees now, and we soon arrive at the spring which is the source of the branch we have been following. The air is heavy with a strong ammonia smell from bird droppings.

Woyi explains that this is a favorite watering place for the woyi. They will be thirsty and hungry as they fly from their roost to the place where they will feed for the day. They will stop here to drink, and we will catch some of them.

The sky in the east is growing lighter now and the few clouds are tinged with shades of pink. Soon, I can see the water of the spring clearly where it runs out from under a rocky ledge to form a pool in the small clearing in the tall trees. The only thing I see which appears unusual is a low, flat topped mound of earth, like a platform, about six feet across, and near the edge of the pool of water. On the side of the mound opposite the pool, is a growth of low bushes. The soft ground around the pool is bare of grass and tracked by the feet of countless birds from yesterday, along with the tracks of a couple of deer and a black bear that passed through during the night.

Woyi shows us how we will catch the pigeons. From the leather pouch he carries, he removes a few handfuls of corn meal and spreads the meal on the flat top of the mound. Then he shows us that the "bushes" beside the mound actually conceal a shallow pit that is large enough for the three of us to lie down. The pit has been covered with a framework of cane, and then covered with brush to form a blind in which we are completely concealed. An opening in the side of the blind next to the platform is screened by a curtain of long grass through which we can see and catch the pigeons, but which keeps them from seeing us.

I ask if we catch the pigeons with our hands, and Woyi replies that we could only catch a few pigeons if we did that, because the flock would see our hands and be frightened away. He shows us the snares we will use to catch the pigeons. Each snare is made from a cane pole about six feet long with a loop of thin sinew on the end. The sinew loop is made so that it will slip, like a lariat rope, and is stiff enough so that the loop stays open and stands out from the pole.

Woyi explains that we will slip the snare poles out on to the top of the mound and wait for a pigeon to begin pecking corn meal from within the loop. Then we will quickly jerk the pole to close the loop on the pigeon's neck and pull the pigeon through the opening into the blind.

I ask if the flopping of the captured pigeon won't scare the others away, but Woyi assures me that the other pigeons will be so busy eating or trying to get a spot to eat that they will pay no attention to the snared bird.

Woyi says we must hurry now because it is full daylight and the pigeons will be coming before long. He takes one of the tame pigeons from the cage and puts a little leather hood over it's head and ties it on with sinew thongs under its head so that the pigeon cannot see. Then he ties a sinew thong to its leg and ties the other end to a thin wooden pole about six feet long that we had carried in with the cane poles. He sets the pigeon on the pole, near the end, and it holds tightly on to the pole with its feet. Woyi explains that, when the pigeon cannot see, it will not release its hold on the pole. He quickly prepares the other tame pigeon on another pole and we crawl into the blind.

I find myself listening intently to the sounds of the flowing water, the songbirds calling, the breeze in the trees and the drone of insects in the air. After awhile, I become aware of another sound from the east, somewhat like the droning insects and the breeze but growing, like a strong wind coming in the distance. The sound grows and Woyi looks toward us with a smile and whispers, "Woyi!"

The sky darkens, as from the approach of rain clouds, and the sound increases to a roar from thousands of beating wings and the loud, clucking and chattering calls of the pigeons. I turn to look through the branches and leaves in the blind above us and see a great, dark, whirling cloud of pigeons descending into the tall trees around our clearing. Soon, every branch and twig is filled with pigeons and the whirling cloud appears unabated as new arrivals search for a place to sit.

Strangely, not one of the thousands of thirsty birds descends to the pool of water to drink. They are wary, and it is as if no one wants to be first. Then I discover the purpose for the blindfolded tame pigeons sitting on the sticks on top of the mound. Woyi moves the pole, and his pigeon flaps its wings to regain its balance on its perch. He motions for us to do the same with our pole and pigeon. The pigeons in the trees see our pigeons on the mound and, reassured that all is safe, they begin to fly down to the pool and drink.

The pigeons came to drink, but they quickly discover the corn meal on top of the mound and they are as hungry as they are thirsty. Some begin to peck the meal which attracts others and, soon, the flat top of the mound is filled with frantically feeding pigeons and the area above it with a cloud of pigeons flying and attempting to find a place to land on the mound.

Woyi slowly withdraws the pole, with his tame decoy pigeon, back into the blind and we do the same. We put the decoys into the cages because they are no longer needed.

Woyi slips his snare pole out and lays it flat on top of the mound among the feeding pigeons and, instantly, some are feeding inside the loop at the end of his pole. He quickly flips and jerks the pole and pulls a flopping pigeon through the grass curtain into the blind. He snaps its neck with his thumb and finger and sticks it, still flopping, into the net bag beside him. In an instant, he has reformed the loop at the end of his pole and he slips it back through the grass curtain and onto the mound. In a few seconds, he pulls another pigeon into the blind.

We slip our pole snare out onto the mound but we quickly learn that catching the pigeons is not as easy and Woyi makes it look. The pigeons are wary and quick and move out of the way when we try to flip the loop over their heads. But after several misses, we catch our first pigeon; by the leg rather than the neck, but it is a catch, nevertheless. After awhile, we are catching them with some consistency, although, Woyi is catching four or five for every one that we catch.

After two hours, our arms ache from catching pigeons, and still the cloud of pigeons above us whirls. Woyi had told us that sometimes a big flock would take as much as three hours to water at the spring. I am wondering if I can hold out for another hour when an unexpected visitor solves my problem.

I see a flash of brown from the corner of my eye and see a bobcat charging from the trees at the edge of the clearing. In an instant he is on the mound and grabs the pigeon that I have snared and am pulling through the grass curtain! For an instant, his face comes through the curtain with my pigeon in his mouth, his yellow eyes look into mine from a distance of one foot, and he growls from deep in his throat! I decide not to argue with him and release my snare pole. He springs from the mound and into the woods with my pigeon in his mouth and my snare pole flopping behind.

Of course, the other pigeons rise in a cloud at the bobcat's charge and now, after your initial surprise, you and Woyi burst into uncontrollable laughter at the expression on my face, which frightens away any remaining pigeons, so our hunt is over for today. It is several minutes before the two of you can control your laughter and my heart starts to beat again. Woyi says he will name me Woyi gakaneha (Woe-yee gah-kah-nay-hah; He gives away the pigeon) and we all three burst into laughter again.

We have over 100 pigeons in our net bags. Another day, Woyi will show us another method of hunting pigeons. But now, we are hungry and thirsty. We drink from the clear water where the spring pours from beneath the rocks because the pigeons have muddied and fouled the water in the pool. We walk to another small clearing, upwind from the spring to get away from the odor of the pigeon droppings. Woyi takes a small clay pot from his pack and, from it, produces a coal of fire which he brought, imbedded in ashes, from his home fire. In the meantime, we select several young pigeons from the bags and clean them. We soon have a fire going and pigeons roasting on green sticks. Then we fill our empty bellies. The flesh of the wild pigeon, and especially a young one, is fat and juicy and fine flavored. After we finish eating, Woyi says the day is cool and the pigeons will not spoil and he feels like a little nap. That sounds like a good idea to me. There is a smooth, soft bed of moss over there that looks just right for me.

CHAPTER 30
THE SPIRITS ARE SPEAKING TO ME THIS MORNING

I leave my house and walk toward the river. My heart is heavy and my spirit as somber as the February landscape around me. My wife and soul-mate, Frankie, is gravely ill and I fear that she will leave me.

I hear a gentle, melodious voice and a bluebird flies before me; his brilliant blue wings and back and rosy breast glow in the morning sun against the gray trees. He flies along before me as I walk, landing on tree branches and talking to me in his soft voice.

"My foolish brother," he says. "You have so little faith. How can you doubt that the spirits love you. They have surrounded you and me with beauty if we only have eyes to see it."

Beside the river, I look for the eagles I often see, who always raise my spirit, but there are no eagles. After days of heavy rain, the river is flooded and muddy and the eagles cannot see the fish, so today they have gone elsewhere to seek clear water. Suddenly, I hear a shrill, piercing voice and a red-shouldered hawk flies across the river and she glows in the morning sun. She lands in the top of a tall sycamore tree on the island in the river and shows me her nest where she will raise her young in the spring.

"My foolish brother," she cries to me. "You have so little faith. How can you doubt that the spirits will protect you. They have not forsaken you and they never will. Each year they protect you and me, as they protected our parents, and will protect our children forever."

I hear a snort, almost like a deer snorts, from the river and see something swimming in the muddy water near the rock ledges where I stand. I first think it is a beaver, hunting a refuge from the flood, but it doesn't swim like a beaver. Then it surfaces with a fish in its mouth and I see that it is an otter, the first one I have ever seen in my river. Their race has been extinct from the Cherokee Nation since long before I was born and now, on this day, this one has returned for me. He sees me where I stand and stretches his neck out of the water for a better look at me, and perhaps to show me his fish.

"My foolish brother," he snorts at me through his nose. "You have so little faith. How can you doubt that the spirits will provide for you. They let me find the fish even when the water is muddy. They have always provided for you and me and they always will."

A loud, beautiful voice rings out from the nearby cane break. A brown wren flies up and perches on the side of a cane stalk, its tail sticking straight up, and its body appearing too small for so large a voice.

"My foolish brother," she scolds me, "You have so little faith. How can you feel unworthy and without

144

purpose. The Eternal One give each of us a voice and a song to sing. The song is truth and beauty and the joy of living! I sing it with my throat, your neighbor with his plow, and you with your pen. Let us sing it every day!"

Following my morning custom, I kneel beside the sacred river, dip my fingers into the water and touch my forehead. Then I pray, "Sagwu Igohidv (Sah-gwoo Ee-goe-hee-duh; Eternal One), gvyadageyuha (guh-yah-dah-gay-you-hah; I love you). Galieliga (Gah-lee-aye-lee-gah; I am happy/thankful). Wado (Wah-doe; Thank You)."

When I return to Frankie's bedside, she asks me why I am smiling. I say, "The spirits spoke to me this morning."

She asks, "What did they say?"

"They say they love us and you are going to be okay."

PS: The events described above occurred on Saturday, February, 22, 1997. Frankie's condition began to improve that day and she completely recovered her normal good health. Her doctors were mystified by her recovery.

The Spirit Stream

There is a Spirit Stream that flows
Through endless space and starry glows
And through it every living thing
The soul of every other knows.

Listen closely and you can bear
The messages from far and near;
Through time and space the themes of life
Are even now converging here.

Into the Spirit Stream there flies
The soul of everything that dies
And every living thing at birth
Out of the Spirit Stream doth rise.

As water drops can vaporize
And fly as vapor through the skies,
Life turns to spirit in the stream
And through the universe it flies.

As vapor changes back to dew,
The spirit will all life renew.
In a great circle without end,
All worlds are sown with life anew.

Those intermingled in the stream
Will realize life's greatest dream:
To be complete, with all things one;
The simple truth of Heaven's scheme.

CHAPTER 31
THE MEDICINE WHEEL

The Medicine Wheel is located high in the Bighorn Mountains of North-Central Wyoming. It is a place few people have even heard of, let alone visited. The Wheel is formed from stones laid on the ground in the shape of a wheel about fifty feet in diameter with twenty eight spokes radiating from a central hub. It lays on the bare top of a mountain, above timberline, and thousands of feet above the floors of the surrounding valleys.

I believe the 28 spokes of the Wheel are related to the four seasons and the mystical member seven; four times seven being 28.

The Medicine Wheel is ancient. The first white people who discovered it and asked the local Native Americans about it were told that it was built by "the ones who came before we were here." Some scientists who have studied the Wheel believe it had astronomical, as well as religious significance. Certain spokes and cairns on the rim line up with the places on the horizon where the sun rises on the spring and fall equinoxes. The spokes could thus mark the seasons, times for return of the buffalo herds, times for planting, festivals, etc.

My son-in-law, Todd Phillips, and I visited the Medicine Wheel in early June of 1992. Snowdrifts still closed the road to the site and we had to leave the car and walk about 1-1/2 miles, crossing several snowfields on the steep mountainside, to reach the Wheel. But, the experience of being there made the effort worthwhile.

My daughter and son-in-law, had visited the site the previous summer, and they had described a strange feeling of awe they had experienced at the Wheel. Now, I experienced similar feelings. Part of it might be attributed to the altitude or the wildness and majesty of the remote scene, but there was an awe and euphoria that went beyond human analysis. I felt it came from being close to the Spirit World.

Many other modem day Native American visitors apparently had the same feelings, because the fence surrounding the Wheel was festooned with prayer bundles, prayer cloths, feathers and other offerings left by worshipers.

No one else had braved the snow drifts, so we were alone in the silence broken only by the sound of the wind and the cries of golden eagles. There was only the majesty of Nature and the Wheel and we felt free from the boundaries of time and the barriers of the modem world. We dreamed awhile in the time and world of our ancient Native American forefathers until the setting sun reminded us that we must come down from the mountain.

My visit to the Medicine Wheel changed me. My spiritual link to all living things and to the Spirit World was amplified. I visualized a Spirit Stream that connects every living thing to every other living thing throughout the universe. I have attempted to describe that connection with the poem on page 146.

CHAPTER 32
THE SEVEN ELEMENTS

Aristotle taught that there are four elements: earth, air, fire and water, and that everything physical is made up of those elements in differing proportions. The concept of four elements influenced European thinking for centuries. Those same four elements played a central role in the thinking of the ancient Cherokees.

The Cherokees believed that the spiritual world was as real, and as important as the physical world. If we are to understand that belief, I believe we need to add three more elements to our list; spirit, life and wisdom for a total of seven elements.

Ama (Ah-mah: Water)

Cherokees referred to the river as Yvwi Ganvhida (Yuh-wee   Gah-nuh-hee-dah; Long Person). The river was considered a living, sacred being that connected all living things. Water was part of everything alive. It was sacred in that it could carry the spirits. It was believed that when a Cherokee died, his or her spirit could enter the river and travel up it to its source at a spring where the spirit could go down the spring to enter the underworld.

The river could also serve as a channel of communication between the spirits of living beings. "Going to water" was a daily ritual of every Cherokee where prayers of thanksgiving and pleas for help were offered. Important occasions such as birth and death, becoming an adult, marriage, war, the hunt, stickball games, etc. all involved going to water as part of the event. The medicine people, shamans, and holy people had an unusual ability to perceive the spiritual communications from the river and send communications to other beings through the river. The healing powers of the water were often part of the treatment of the sick.

Ajila (Ah-jee-lah: Fire)

In the Cherokee cosmology, there are two kinds of fire; red fire (ah-jee-lah gee-gah-gay) and white fire (ah-jee-lah oo-nay-gah). Looking at fire in this way allows us to relate it to the Spirit World. The red fire is related to power and success in competitions such as war, games or new beginnings. The red paths were said to cross at the fire built for the "war" dance. The red paths stretched to the east, south, west and north to the ends of the earth.

The white fire is related to wisdom, peace and harmony. The white paths were said to cross at the fire built for the "peace" dance. The white paths stretched in four directions to the ends of the earth.

Of course, normal, everyday fire is a mixture of red and white as normal, everyday life is a mixture of seeking a balance between achievement and peace.

150

Elohi (Aye-loe-hee: Earth)

The element earth is one of the four elements that make up the physical universe. Most things in the physical world contain all four elements, in varying proportions. For example, rocks contain mostly earth and smaller proportions of the other three physical elements. Rocks also contain the spiritual elements in varying proportions. Rocks have spirit, but, evidently, little life. I'm not sure yet how much wisdom rocks have. A person, on the other hand, contains less earth, and more of the other three physical elements than does a rock. A person also contains the spiritual elements in varying proportions.

According to one Cherokee legend, in the beginning, all was water. Then Doyanisi (Doe-yah-nee-see; Beaver's Grandchild), the little water beetle, darted about over the water but could find no firm place to rest. Then it dived beneath the water and brought up a little mud, which began to grow until it became the island we call earth.

Unole (Oo-noe-lay: Air)

The Cherokee word, Unole, means air moving, from a breeze to a tornado. Air is hard to detect, with our normal senses, unless it is moving. We detect air by feeling the breeze on our face or seeing the leaves blowing or seeing the ripples on the water.

Air is one of the four physical elements, and is found in varying proportions in all physical things. Air is necessary for most life, both plant and animal. Air is also connected to the spirit. The concept of the four winds is common to many Native American cultures. Many ceremonies involve addressing the four winds which carry messages to or from the Spirit World.

Adanto (Ah-dah-nuh-toe: Spirit)

I believe there is a spiritual component to every physical thing in the universe. I believe the spirit is just as real as the physical thing we can see or touch, although, we usually can't detect spirit with our normal senses. Spirit is like the wind. We can't see the wind, but we detect its presence by feeling it on our skin or seeing it blow the leaves or ripple the water. We detect spirit by feeling it on our intuition and through its affect on interactions in our lives. I know that spirit is involved when "coincidences" in my life happen too frequently to be explained by mere chance.

I think of the Spirit World as existing in at least two domains; the domain which lies beyond this life and the domain which is around and within each of us and every other living or nonliving thing in the universe.

The domain that lies beyond this life is entirely spirit. Here live the spiritual counterparts of every physical thing on earth. The ancient Cherokees believed that many of those spiritual beings are white.

I conceptualize the other spiritual domain as existing within and among living and non-living things. The ancient Cherokees believed in the interaction of the spirits of all things. Mankind was not higher than the other creatures or plants in spirit or in wisdom.

Ulenitohv (Uh-lay-nee-toe-huh: Life)

Life, like spirit, is usually not detected by our normal senses but by our intuition and, indirectly, through the observed behavior of living things. As with the other elements, differing amounts of life are displayed by different physical things. A rock displays none of this element while my grandchildren display a lot of this element.

When a physical thing is animated by spirit, life begins. When the spirit leaves the physical thing, life ends.

Akto^uhhisdi (Ahk-toe^uh-hee-sdee: Wisdom)

Wisdom is one of the three spiritual elements. It relates to insight; the ability to discern inner qualities and relationships. It manifests itself through good sense and judgment; the ability to perceive truth.

I have always marveled at the wisdom of young children. Many have an innate ability to discern the inner qualities of the people around them and to know the truth in spite of what we adults tell them.

Wisdom does not automatically develop as a person becomes an adult and grows older. Guidance is necessary for the development of wisdom. I believe that guidance is best when it comes from the spirits speaking directly to us rather than through a third party. I have met few truly wise people whose primary guidance came from the dominant religions or institutions of higher learning of the world. In my experience, an educated person is often not a wise person. In fact, most of the truly wise people I have known had little formal education.

The person who is merely educated, but lacks wisdom, quotes what other people think, while the wise person says what he or she thinks, and his or her words reflect insight and truth. The wise people I have met have been formed by contact with nature, good people in their everyday life and contact with the Spirit World through their inner voice. Their perception is focused on the good and the beautiful in life. They keep an open mind to the opinions of all people, but they primarily rely on the spirits, speaking to them through their own inner voice, to show them the path to wisdom.

153

CHAPTER 33
THROWING ROCKS

Usually, when we think of primitive weapons that can kill at a distance, we think of bows and arrows, blowguns, spears, atlatls, etc. But in the hands of a skilled thrower, a chunk of rock can be a deadly weapon. I have found little written about the thrown rock as a weapon, other than the famous story of David and Goliath.

My father was born in the Cherokee Nation in Indian Territory in 1904. During his prime, he was one of the best rock throwers and one of the best trackers in the Cherokee Nation.

Rock throwing is a time-honored pastime among the Cherokees. My father, like other Cherokee children growing up in rural poverty, had no athletic fields or even a ball to throw, so he threw the flint rocks that cover the ground almost everywhere in the Cherokee Nation. He had no gun or ammunition, and, being orphaned at an early age, no one to make him a bow and arrows, so he hunted with rocks. This was nothing unusual because most of the people he knew threw rocks. He and other boys and some girls regularly killed squirrels, rabbits, quail and other small game with thrown rocks.

The tradition continued while I was a boy growing up in the Cherokee Nation. Whether I was by myself or with other boys walking a rocky country road or along a stream I was constantly throwing rocks at knots on trees or posts, sticks floating on the water, birds, or anything that presented a likely target. Our greatest delight was finding a can which we would keep constantly jumping from hits by rocks. By the time I was a teen, I could throw hard and would seldom miss my target, but my father could throw with much greater speed and accuracy, and he was middle aged.

The story is told in our family that once, when my father was a young man, he borrowed a mule from his brother-in-law, Marve Pilcher, to plow a field on his land allotment. The contrary mule kept rearing, kicking, and doing everything except pulling the plow. Finally, my father tired of it and, as the mule reared, my father quickly reached down and picked up a rock the size of a hen's egg, threw it and hit the mule behind the ear. The mule fell like it had been shot and lay on its side with its legs sticking straight out and quivering!

My father thought he had killed the mule, and was wondering how he would explain it to Uncle Marve. But after a couple of minutes, the mule started moving, got up, shook itself and acted like it was ready to work. My relieved and delighted father started plowing, but, as the dazed mule regained its senses, it again started rearing. My father reached down for another rock, hit the rearing mule in exactly the same spot as before with exactly the same result!

Again he stood looking down on the quivering mule, wondering if he had killed it. Again, the mule revived after a few minutes and it had evidently gotten the message, because my father said he had no more trouble with the mule.

I first heard that story about my father and the mule as a young child and later, when I heard the story of David killing Goliath with a stone, I remember thinking "Pa could have done that and he wouldn't have needed no sling!"

The famous Cookson Hills, which were a sanctuary for outlaws before Indian Territory became the state of Oklahoma, lie within the Cherokee Nation. The story is told about two outlaws who got into an argument over a card game. One went outside the house, gathered up several rocks, and waited for the other to come outside. When the other one appeared, he had a revolver, but the one with the rocks didn't feel at a disadvantage, so they started firing away at one another; the one on the porch with his pistol and the one in the yard with rocks. The one with the revolver soon emptied it, hitting nothing while receiving several painful injuries from rocks. What's more, he was out of bullets, while the other man had an unlimited supply of rocks.

He threw his pistol at his assailant and managed to get back into the house and lock the door. He crouched behind the bed while the rock thrower broke all the windows in the house and triumphantly rode away.

I remember when I was a small child we had a big red rooster that would chase me whenever he could. One day he caught me by surprise and flogged me, cutting my knee with one of his spurs and scaring me half to death. I screamed and my father came running down the hill from the barn. The rooster, strongly suspecting he was in big trouble, ran down the hill to the garden fence, turned to the right and ran along the fence with his neck stretched out and as fast as he could go. My father checked to see if I was badly hurt, quickly picked up a rock, threw and hit the running rooster perfectly in the head. The rooster flopped around a lot while dying and I enjoyed every flop. The next day, I enjoyed eating him in a pot of dumplings.

The tradition of throwing among the Cherokees produced a number of good baseball players, in later years when baseball diamonds were built in many communities and equipment became available. I became a fair pitcher myself, although, I was never good enough to play professional baseball. But, several of my teammates did play professional baseball.

I have heard the story about a scout from a professional baseball team who heard about the throwing ability of one Cherokee boy and came to his house. The boy's parents told the scout the boy was out in the woods, and the scout went to look for him. He saw a boy at a distance, throwing a rock up into a tall tree, and, a second later, a dead squirrel came tumbling from the tree. The scout approached and told the boy what a fantastic throw that had been, but he was evidently not the boy the scout was seeking because the boy he wanted was left-handed.

"I am left-handed," the boy said.

"But, I just saw you throw right handed at that squirrel," the scout said.

"Oh," the boy explained, "I threw right handed because, when I throw left handed, I tear up the squirrels too bad."

CHAPTER 34
ENTERTAINMENT ON THE FARM

When I was a boy growing up a farm in the Cherokee Nation in the 1940's and 1950's, I usually had to invent my own entertainment. Our house did not have electricity, indoor plumbing or air conditioning. We had no TV, in fact, the first one I ever saw was when I was in high school. We had a battery-powered radio that was used sparingly to conserve the expensive battery. I liked to read, but my mother wouldn't let me read a lot by lamplight for fear I would harm my eyes. So, I spent a lot of time in the out-of-doors. The Cherokee Nation is blessed by many rocks, and I loved to throw rocks. Our house was near the clear, spring-fed Barren Fork Creek where I loved to swim and fish in the summer, and gig fish in the winter.

We normally had few visitors. Our nearest neighbors, who had kids, lived about two miles from our house. I seldom got to go to other kids' houses to spend a day or a night, nor did other kids come to visit me. There were morning and evening chores to be done every day. Through nine months of the year, I was in school five days each week. Most of the summer days were filled with hoeing weeds in the corn fields and mowing and baling hay. Work on a farm does not stop for weekends either. Sunday mornings, after the morning chores, we went to church, but Sunday afternoon was often spent doctoring a sick animal or taking care of some other emergency; then came the evening chores.

Of course, my folks would take time, whenever possible, to go fishing, picnicking or visiting neighbors or kin-folks. Sometimes, we would go to a pie supper at the school when the school needed to raise money for something.

At the pie suppers and other gatherings we attended, I got the chance to play with other kids. Of course, I got to play with other kids at school during recess, but that wasn't nearly as much fun as playing at night, among the big trees in the dark school yard, while the adults were all inside bidding on pies and visiting. We would get up a game of "Kick the Can" or "Go in and out the window" and time seemed to stand still. I got my first kiss during a game of "Go in and out the Window", and it changed my opinion of girls. I still had no idea what they were good for, but I sensed they were not as useless as I had always thought.

But, my times spent with other children were relatively few, and I learned to enjoy being by myself. I learned to play the harmonica and played it as I walked to and from school and during my chores at home. I learned to hunt and made some spending money hunting possums at night during the winter.

Sometimes, my folks let me ride our little mare, Cricket, to the country store that was a few miles from our house. There, I would watch and listen to the old men playing checkers in the feed room at the back of the store. It was there that I first met Kawaya. After that, I spent some of my free time with him. He taught me many things about the old Cherokee way and that learning could be as much fun as play.

Christmas was always a happy time. We seldom had snow at Christmas, so, when we had a white Christmas, it was a special thing. I remember one white Christmas in particular; it was during World War II, and I was eight or nine years old. My older, half-brother came home from the navy with stories about his time in the Pacific and he brought me a box of .410 gauge shotgun shells. Ammunition was impossible to get, because of the war, and I hadn't had any shells for my little .410 for a year. I don't know how he got the shells, but he did. There was six inches of snow on the ground and more was falling.

After dinner, the "men" (including me!) went out to hunt rabbits in the snow. I carried the only gun, the others just wanted to watch me. We would get on a rabbit track in the snow and follow it until we jumped the rabbit, and I would shoot it with my .410. I got four rabbits, a couple of squirrels and three quail without missing a shot. My brother was amazed at how I could shoot, and my father bragged on me. When we got home, we cleaned the game, my mother cooked it, and we all had supper together. It was one of the best days of my life.

CHAPTER 35
POSSUM SEX

As a boy in the 1940's and 50's, I hunted opossums (or "possums", as we called them) as a source of spending money. During the cold months, the hides were worth about 15 cents apiece. I had a feist dog, named Cat, that would tree about anything, and on a good night in the hills and bottoms along Barren Fork Creek, Cat and I might get three or four possums. That was usually on Friday or Saturday night, since my folks wouldn't let me hunt on school nights. Then the next day, I would spend two or three hours skinning the possums and stretching the hides. I was making about 10 cents an hour or less, but I considered that pretty good money. Besides, I loved to hunt.

I hunted alone, and just carried a coal-oil lantern and a tow sack. When Cat would tree a possum, perhaps a quarter-mile away through the dark woods, I would run to where he was treed. Then, I climbed the tree and caught the possum, which wasn't very hard to do, because the possum usually didn't climb very high when treed; often just going out on the first side limb. Often, the tree was a small persimmon tree, the fruit of which is the possum's first love. I would climb up, thump the possum a time or two with a stick until he sulled-up, and then carry or drop his seemingly lifeless body to the ground. I would sack him up and then Cat would take off to hunt another possum.

Toward the end of a successful hunt, I would have several live possums in my tow sack. Carrying a sack with three or four possums that hated each

163

other, and carrying a lantern, was a challenge for a ten-year-old boy.

I had built cages In which I could keep the possums alive if I couldn't skin them right away. So, I had a lot of opportunity to observe possums and learn their strange ways, and the strangest of all was their sex life.

Somebody told me that possums mate through the nose. Being an average curious boy, I thought that possums mating through the nose was something I would like to see. I caged numberless pairs of males and females together, and observed with infinite patience.

Sometimes, my mother would come by the possum cages, and say, "Al, why do you spend so much time out here watching those crazy possums? If you don't stop, you are going to go crazy yourself!"

Of course, as mothers always do, she exaggerated the danger. I suffered no ill effects, except a tendency to faint whenever a teacher spoke sharply to me, and I simply could not pass up a persimmon tree.

Now, back to my observations of the amorous possums: Mostly they would grin, hiss and growl at each other from opposite comers of the cage, and, to my great disappointment, if any ever mated, nasal or otherwise, I didn't see it.

My curiosity was further aroused by the discovery that the young possums, which I would sometimes find in the female's pouch in late February (I always released females carrying young), were unbelievably tiny, and so poorly developed they looked like tiny pinkish worms, each fastened securely to a teat inside the pouch.

Further observation and some reading in the school library revealed to me that the sex life of the possum was even more strange and wonderful than some of the old stories I had heard. Possums don't

164

mate through the nose, but in the more traditional manner. However, from that point on, things become rather strange. As many as 20 to 40 eggs may be fertilized, they gestate for only 13 days, and then they are born!

Each baby is a tiny blind lump of tissue less than 1/2 inch long and weighing 1/175 ounce! About the only noticeable details are a pair of front limbs with well formed claws. The survival of each tiny creature depends upon its ability to crawl up the mother's fur from the birth canal to the pouch, and attach itself to one of the 13 teats in the pouch. Those who do not make the climb, or find all the teats taken, do not survive.

Those baby possums that manage to attach themselves to a teat in the pouch do not relinquish their hold for about 60 days; indeed, the pouch becomes a second womb, and they are like embryos fastened inside. The mother can open the pouch to sun her young, or tightly close it to keep them warm and dry even when she swims. At about 60 days of age, the young are about the size of mice. They open their eyes, and release their hold on the teat for the first time. At about 80 days of age, they can control their body temperature, and leave the pouch for short periods. The young stay with their mother for about 100 days, and when they get too large to all fit in the pouch at one time, some ride on her back, while others ride In the pouch.

I told you it was a strange and wonderful story! So, the next time you are at a tea party or something, and the topic of possum sex comes up in the conversation, and somebody mentions that possums mate through the nose-- you stop them and say, "Hey, wait a minute. Let me tell you what really happens. This in one instance where truth is stranger than fiction!"

CHAPTER 36
SEQUOYAH AND THE CHEROKEE SYLLABARY

In 1821, after twelve years of work on attempting to develop a written language for the Cherokees, Sequoyah's syllabary was accepted by the Council of the Cherokee Nation. In a span of a little more than a year from the acceptance of the syllabary, thousands of previously illiterate Cherokees were able to read and write their own language, and within two or three years, the literacy rate in the Cherokee Nation was probably higher than the literacy rate in the United States today. This is the only instance in history of a person single-handedly developing a system for writing a spoken language.

These facts are remarkable in themselves, but when the circumstances surrounding Sequoyah's life, and his development of the syllabary are considered, the story is truly amazing. The development of the syllabary would have been a remarkable feat for a scholar, working in a supportive academic environment, and building on the systems of writing of previous scholars. But Sequoyah was illiterate, with no concept of language structure or how language could be represented by symbols.

He saw that the white man could put on paper something which another white man could understand. Most of Sequoyah's peers felt that the white man was using witchcraft, or that writing was a gift that the creator gave only to the white man. But Sequoyah said he did not believe that it was witchcraft or a special gift, but that the marks on the paper stood for words. He reasoned that if the white man could talk on paper, then the Cherokee should be able to talk on paper, and he resolved to make that possible.

After he began work on a written language, he neglected his regular work and domestic duties, and spent most of his time alone in the woods or in a small cabin where he worked. His friends, associates and even family members began to wonder if he was possessed by devils. A hunter told of seeing Sequoyah in the woods, sitting on the ground playing like a child with pieces of wood he had chopped from a tree. When the hunter spoke to him, Sequoyah did not hear or look up; he was so intent at his play. Others saw him in the woods or along the stream making odd little marks on rocks, using paint rocks as pencils, or carving marks in wood with his knife. Many of his former friends avoided him, and others openly ridiculed him.

After he had been working on his written language for two years, someone lured him from his little work cabin and burned it along with all his work, evidently in an attempt to put a stop to his foolishness, and perhaps return him to sanity. Undaunted, he started again.

Sequoyah first attempted to design a symbol for each word, using a form of pictograph like those used to write Chinese. He soon found that this would result in thousands of characters. He then received a true stroke of genius; a phonetic approach in which he eventually found that 84 characters could represent all the syllables of the Cherokee language. The system was so simple and straight-forward that a speaker of Cherokee could often learn to read and write in less than a day.

A legend is told among the Cherokees about how Sequoyah received this inspiration, and I will relate it to you now.

Legend of the White Butterfly

Sequoyah had four sons and one daughter and the little girl, Nancy, was the apple of his eye. His work on a written language had cost him his friends and his standing in the community, but in Nancy he still found joy. Then Nancy was taken gravely ill, and in two or three days, she died and Sequoyah's will to continue seemed to die with her.

One morning after a night of rain, Sequoyah arose and asked his wife, Sallie, to fix him some sofka to eat. Sallie was glad to do this because he hadn't eaten anything for days in grief over Nancy's death. He said that he and the boy were going up on the mountain. So after they ate, he and the boy departed.

They were halfway up the mountain when Sequoyah's strength failed, and he told the boy he must rest. A little stream of clear water about two feet deep flowed down the mountain, and Sequoyah drank from the stream and then laid down in the shade of a tree beside the stream, while the boy laid down nearby. Sequoyah soon fell asleep, but the boy remained awake, watching the little fish playing in a clear pool in the stream.

Suddenly, the boy was surprised to see a large white butterfly come out of the water, fly around the sleeping Sequoyah's head several times, and then alight on his chin. The white butterfly sat there for awhile, and then arose and flew around Sequoyah's head two or three more times before it flew back to the stream and disappeared into the water.

Presently, Sequoyah awoke. He told the boy that he had found his little girl that he had lost. Little Nancy had appeared to him in a dream. "See here what she brought me," he said and in his hand was a flat stone and a "pencil", and the Cherokee syllabary was written on the stone. "She showed me how to write the Cherokee language, and told me to teach the writing to all my grandchildren through the world."

With the acceptance of the Cherokee Syllabary, Sequoyah was transformed almost overnight from an outcast and suspected witch to a celebrity, teacher and revered leader. He was recognized as a true genius, and he was honored beyond the Cherokee Nation to the entire United States and the world. The giant redwood trees of California are named Sequoyah in his honor.

In the Sequoyah Syllabary which follows, the symbol for each syllable is shown and its sound is shown in small English letters to the right of the symbol. For example, the first symbol, which resembles the English letter "D", has the sound "a". Consonants used in Cherokee speech are pronounced the same as in English. The vowels are "a" (sounds like ah), "e" (sounds like aye), "i" (sounds like ee), "o" (sounds like owe), "u" (sounds like oo), and "v" (sounds like the uh in h<u>uh</u>).

SEQUOYAH SYLLABARY

D a	R e	T i	Ꮔ o	Ꮕ u	i v
Ꮝ ga / Ꮣ ka	Ꮐ ge	Ꮩ gi	A go	J gu	E gv
Ꮲ ha	Ꮶ he	Ꮙ hi	Ꮚ ho	Ꮁ hu	Ꮣ hv
W la	Ꮯ le	Ꮲ li	Ꮆ lo	M lu	Ꮴ lv
Ꮉ ma	Ꮄ me	H mi	Ꮒ mo	Ꮠ mu	
Ꮻ na / Ꮏ hna	Ꮑ ne	Ꮆ ni	Z no	Ꮕ nu	Ꮻ nv
Ꮖ gwa	Ꮼ gwe	Ꮘ gwi	Ꮺ gwo	Ꮽ gwu	Ꮿ gwv
Ꮶ sa / Ꮝ s	4 se	Ꮞ si	Ꮠ so	Ꮡ su	R sv
Ꮭ da / W ta	Ꮥ de / Ꮦ te	Ꭻ di / Ꮧ ti	V do	S du	Ꮷ dv
Ꮬ tla / Ꮣ dla	L tle	C tli	Ꮸ tlo	Ꮹ tlu	P tlv
Ꮐ ja	Ꮮ je	Ꮵ ji	K jo	Ꮷ ju	Ꮸ jv
Ꮐ wa	Ꮺ we	Ꮻ wi	Ꮼ wo	Ꮽ wu	Ꮾ wv
Ꮿ ya	Ᏸ ye	Ᏹ yi	Ᏺ yo	Ᏻ yu	B yv

CHAPTER 37
THE SEARCH FOR SEQUOYAH'S TOMB

I, Tsquayi, member of the Cherokee Nation, herein write my true account of my experiences and impressions relating to my trip to Mexico for the purpose of evaluating the recently discovered site believed to be the lost tomb of Sequoyah.

The Search for Sequoyah: A Cherokee Odyssey

A famous legend of the Aztecs tells of their travels from the north, seeking a homeland. A sign was foretold that would show them where they were to build their city. The sign would be an eagle, eating a snake atop a cactus. Finally, on a small island in a lake, they saw the sign, exactly as foretold, and there they built their capitol, the site of the present day Mexico City.

In March of 2001, three signs were revealed to me that related to the Cherokees' ongoing search for the lost grave of Sequoyah. The signs were a white bear, a red bird, and a rattlesnake. I believe the appearance of those signs, along with other evidence, showed that the site we found is the grave of Sequoyah.

In the following pages, I will present some background information, my personal experiences on the trip to Mexico on which the signs appeared and my interpretation of the meaning of each sign.

Background

In November of 2000, I was contacted by Dr. Charles Rogers of Brownsville, Texas. Dr. Rogers operates a medical clinic in Matamoras, Mexico. He was interested in buying a Cherokee bow that had been made for me by the Cherokee bowyer, Alex England. I sold him the bow, along with another Cherokee bow that I made several years ago. I also made him ten ceremonial Cherokee cane arrows, with flint points, for each bow. I did not know it at the time, but, those bows and arrows would play a part in the search for Sequoyah's grave.

In December, Dr. Rogers, his wife Sheron, their 13 year old son, Charles, and Dr. Roger's 86 year old mother, Mary, came through Tahlequah and met with my wife, Frankie, and me. They were searching for their Cherokee roots, primarily through Dr. Roger's Cherokee great-grandmother, Mary Price.

Shortly thereafter, during his research into Cherokee history and genealogy, Dr. Rogers became intrigued by the story of Sequoyah's final journey, into Mexico, in 1843, to convince some Cherokees living there to return to the Cherokee Nation in Indian Territory (now Oklahoma). Sequoyah was accompanied on the journey by his son, Tessee, and a man known as The Worm. Sequoyah, who was seventy-three years old at the time, accomplished his mission, but became ill, died and was buried in

174

Mexico. Several expeditions during the twentieth century have attempted to locate his lost tomb. In 1953, an expedition accompanied by Cherokee Chief, W.W. Keeler, with the intent finding and returning the remains of Sequoyah to the Cherokee Nation, found and excavated two graves, but neither contained the remains of Sequoyah.

Dr. Rogers has many resources in Mexico and believed he could find Sequoyah's lost grave. He asked me to assist in the search and we consulted, almost daily, by phone. I have difficulty describing my role in the search. Charles (we were on a first name basis by then) would tell me, almost daily, about the findings of his workers, two Mexican women who work in his clinic, that went out in search for information through interviews with local people, historians, government officials, and written records from many sources. Sometimes, he would call and let me listen to the workers as he debriefed them about the day's findings. I would listen and then offer comments on what I heard. Often, Charles would tell me that my comments gave him ideas for new directions in his search or verified his own conviction as to the worth of certain information. At first, he was searching near the town of San Fernando, south of Matamoras, Mexico. After one of our conversations, he changed the search area to an area of Mexico near Eagle Pass, Texas.

Dr. Rogers, his wife, Sheron, his mother, Mary, and his son, Charles, made a trip to the area to check out historical records and oral statements that a Cherokee village had been located at or near the present-day town of Zaragoza, Mexico. They checked out an old mission and located some graves with markings that looked like Cherokee writing. As a test of the location, son Charles (I will henceforth refer to him as "little" Charles) shot a ceremonial arrow into the air, believing that it would show the way to the

175

grave. When Charles told me about it later, he said, "The arrow did not come back to the earth!" It had stuck through a small tree limb, the size of a finger, above the ground. They took that as a sign that the grave was not in that area.

Later, they located the ranch that had been visited by the Keeler expedition in 1953. The ranch is owned by Epigmenio and Gloria Rodriguez and has been in their family since the 1700's. The Rodriguezes told stories, that had been handed down through their family, of the Cherokees who lived in the area and of Sequoyah's son and a friend, who came looking for horses since theirs had been stolen in Texas. The two Cherokees had a good eye for horses, selecting their best Arabian horses, and they left immediately to return to where they had left Sequoyah in Texas. Later, they returned, with Sequoyah.

They told another story about Sequoyah and a group of Cherokees being arrested by soldiers from the United States and escorted out of Mexico on the way to the Cherokee Nation. But Sequoyah escaped and returned to the Cherokee town in Mexico. The Rodriguez family hid him in a cave from the soldiers and later, when he became ill and died, he was buried in the cave. Another story related that the ill Sequoyah went into the cave and walled it up behind him, literally burying himself. The Rodriguez family and other Cherokees who remained in Mexico kept the location of the cave secret for more than 150 years, until the arrival of Charles and his family. They said there was a legend among the Cherokees that a child would come to show the way to Sequoyah's grave.

Gloria remembers when, as a girl, a group of Cherokees from Oklahoma came looking for Sequoyah with various maps and information. They asked Gloria's grandmother, Octavia Salinas, what she knew about Sequoyah and where he was buried. She did not trust their mannerisms and they had no child with them so she told them, "No, I don't know anything about it. The land has changed much over the years." Later, someone showed the group from Oklahoma a cemetery where Cherokees were buried and they dug up two of the graves. But the family did not show them the cave where they knew the remains of Sequoyah were buried.

Charles asked why the family would not tell others the location of the cave, but now, they were telling him. Gloria said that, a few days before Charles and his family arrived, she had a vision and saw the face of Charles. She recognized him immediately when she saw him. Also, "Little" Charles was with his father, mother and grandmother when they went to the ranch fulfilling the prophesy that a child would show the way. Incidentally, Charles had not heard of the legend about the child before he and his family met with Epigmenio and Gloria.

Gloria and Epigmenio took Charles and his family to the cave. They all went in and said they felt a great peace in the cave. After being in the cave about 45 minutes, "Little" Charles was looking around and said, "What's this?" He had found some markings on the wall that no one had noticed before. They appeared to be man made and the find seemed to provide further fulfillment of the legend of a child finding the burial place.

Charles arranged for a group of about thirty people, including my wife Frankie and me, to visit the ranch and the cave on March 17, 2001. Charles financed the entire expedition, not for any personal gain, but out of his great generosity and his love for the Cherokee people. All that he asked of us was that we experience the place, listen to and evaluate the stories of Gloria and Epigmenio Rodriguez and ask them any questions we wished. Frankie and I are grateful to Charles for the opportunity to share in that wonderful experience.

The Trip

On Thursday, March 15, 2001, the day before we left on our trip, I drove from our home in the Cherokee Nation to the Tsalagi Heritage Center, a few miles away, to pick up some shell shackles that Frankie and I were borrowing for a demonstration stomp dance that Jonathan and Rose Hook would conduct at the Rodriguez ranch. In the Heritage Center grounds, I was suddenly aware of three trees growing from the ground like three spread fingers on a hand. They somehow stood out from the other trees around them. The spirits spoke to me and said that, on the coming trip, I would see a sign that involved three things. I was not told the significance of the sign, but I hoped I would realize its significance when I saw it.

On Friday, March 16, 2001, Frankie and I flew to San Antonio and caught a ride with Gregg and Lari Howard from there to Eagle Pass. Gregg, a Cherokee language teacher and storyteller who lives in Texas, had been invited by Charles to join our expedition. On the three hour drive, I kept looking for the sign-- perhaps three hawks or ravens or something else, but nothing stood out. We met the others who were part of the expedition at the Holiday Inn Express in Eagle Pass.

The next morning, Saturday, March 17, 2001, we took a bus to the border, transferred to another bus in Mexico and began our 35 mile trip to Zaragoza. The bus driver was a large, jolly man who wheeled the big Mercedes bus through the narrow streets of the Mexican towns as if it were a skateboard. Everyone on the bus was in a festive mood. Frankie and I felt like we were living an Indiana Jones movie.

Suddenly, right before me, was the sign! On the dashboard of the bus, right in front of our jolly driver, was a jolly little white bear. Its head was attached to its body by a spring so that the head bounced and shook on the bumpy road, giving the appearance that it was having as much fun as I was! I asked the driver, in my poor Spanish, if it was indeed a white bear. He flashed me a grin over his shoulder and said, "Si!"

It was then that I realized that I was not to see a sign that involved three things but, instead, three signs. The white bear; my Cherokee name, my Spirit Animal and my guide on my Spirit Path, showed me that I was meant to be there at that time, in that place and going to the place where I was going. Up until that time, neither Frankie nor I were convinced that we deserved the honor of going on the trip. At that time, although I still did not fully understand my role, I knew that I was supposed to be on the trip.

Epigmenio Rodriguez, the owner of the ranch where the cave is located, met our bus along the way and guided us through the town of Zaragoza and then out to the ranch. He first took us through a field to a place where warm sulfur water gushes from the ground to form a small stream. Ghostly whirls of mist arose from the water into the unusually cold air. Nearby was the ruins of an adobe building which was the house where his wife, Gloria, lived as a girl.

Gloria and Epigmenio stood in front of our group and told us some of the family stories relating to Sequoyah and the Cherokees who lived in the area. After they had finished, we had the opportunity to question them. They answered every question in an honest, unrehearsed manner.

Frankie and I introduced ourselves to them and told them that we came from the Cherokee Nation in Oklahoma and that Frankie is the great-great-great granddaughter of Chief John Ross, who asked

Sequoyah to go on the trip to Mexico. We thanked them for the opportunity to visit the site and for their family helping Sequoyah and the Cherokees and for guarding the gravesite all those years.

Next, we reboarded the bus and soon arrived at the Rodriguez Ranch Headquarters where we found a fiesta waiting for us. Near a huge tent and portable toilets brought in for the occasion, a Mexican cook was cutting up the meat of a freshly killed goat to prepare cabrito along with chili, tortillas, and corn fritters. Boxes of styrofoam containers of barbecued meat, beans and potato salad had been brought, on the bus, with us from Eagle Pass. A mariachi band and a cowboy doing rope tricks provided entertainment while we ate. It was indeed a joyful occasion which was not diminished by the unusually cold and damp weather. After we ate, everyone huddled close to several small fires for the warmth of the flames and the good people there.

Someone said, "Look at the red bird!" Someone else said, "It's a cardinal." I looked up from gazing into the flames and saw a beautiful red bird sitting on the nearby wire fence. It flew down to the ground, then back onto the fence several times. The red bird was the second sign. I did not tell the others that it was a sign or the significance of the red bird as a sign. The red bird signifies truth. Other birds are camouflaged and hide themselves. But the red bird stands out, showing his true self for all to see, regardless of the risk. Whether bird or man, he that speaks the truth and does not practice deceit puts himself at risk.

I believe the sign of the red bird was related to the Rodriguez family. We looked into their eyes and their hearts as they spoke and saw that their words were true. Epigmenio, Gloria and their three sons were honest, open, spontaneous, gracious people who welcomed us to their home like lost relations.

180

They knew that disclosing the secret that had been kept in their family for over 150 years was not without risk. There was the risk that the grave could be violated and risk that their privacy and peace could be disturbed. I believe they did it because of their trust in Charles and his family and their belief that the time had come for the Cherokee people to know the final resting place of the great Sequoyah.

While the remainder of the group were entertained by riding horses, shooting bows and arrows, or sitting around the fires visiting, Charles began taking small groups, by car, to the cave. Frankie and I were in the first group, along with Jonathan and Rose Hook, Chief D.L. Hicks, Gregg and Lari Howard, Epigmenio and Gloria Rodriguez, and Charles.

The cave is located in a flat, brush-covered area and was invisible until we were within a few yards of it. There is a rock strewn depression, about 20 yards across and 6 feet deep at the lowest point, in the level ground and the cave entrance is in one side of the depression. The cave entrance is about 2-1/2 or 3 feet high and about 4 feet wide. Jonathan performed a cleansing ceremony with burning cedar to sanctify the cave and those who would enter. Then we prepared to enter the cave.

Charles went to the entrance first, knelt before it and thrust his Cherokee bow back into the cave. He rattled it against the walls and floor on both sides of the opening, figuring that any resident rattlesnakes would rattle so that we could hear them. Satisfied that the way was clear, he crawled into the entrance and called for the rest of us to follow.

I thought there might not be enough room inside for the entire group, so Frankie and I held back to let the others go first. Then, I realized that I had a strange reluctance to going into the cave. I am not particularly afraid of snakes or caves but, I felt an apprehension about going in. I looked at Frankie and she was experiencing the same feelings. Then, the last person in was calling for us to come on in, that there was plenty of room. So I went down to the entrance, with Frankie close behind, and began crawling into the cave.

Inside, I could dimly see people sitting on the floor of the cave in the dark, lit only from the light through the entrance. "Does anyone have a flashlight?" someone asked. I answered that I had one, since I always carry a small flashlight and my Leatherman Tool on my belt when I go adventuring, which is almost every day.

I turned on my flashlight and shined it around. On my right, near the floor, a crevice went back into the wall that was big enough for several rattlesnakes. About shoulder high, there was another crevice that went deep back into the cave wall. I moved the light to the wall on the left side and far back in another crevice near the ceiling, I saw the third sign. I saw its eye first, shining faintly in the flashlight beam, then I made out the head and body of a rattlesnake. I said, "I don't want to spoil the mood of the moment, but I see a snake." Chief Hicks, who was sitting just below the crevice asked me, "Is it close to me?" "Right over your head," I answered.

There wasn't much argument or discussion about what we should do next, although, I did hear one comment about "Al and his damned flashlight!" Frankie was already kicking rocks against my back on her way out and Charles said, "One at a time, everybody out!" He could have saved his breath.

When the cave was cleared, Charles wanted me to show him the snake. I went back in and the snake had not moved. Strangely, I felt less apprehensive than I had felt the first time; the snake didn't bother me as much as the crowd of people. Charles had his bow and said he would stand guard and hit the snake if it came out while I crawled back and looked at the rest of the cave. I didn't want to miss the opportunity to see all of the cave, so, I crawled toward the back wall.

The room we were in was about 10 or 12 feet across, about 5 feet high in the center and appeared to be a natural cave. On the back wall, opposite the entrance, there was another opening and a smaller room, perhaps 8 feet across, that appeared to have been dug. The floor of the smaller room was dirt, different from the rock and dirt of the cave walls and ceiling, that I would guess was brought in from outside. I believe that dirt was brought in to cover the remains of Sequoyah. Then, I crawled back to the cave entrance and left my flashlight with Charles who watched the snake while several other people entered to see the cave and the snake.

After the viewing was complete, I performed a ceremony near the entrance of the cave. A few days before leaving on our trip, Frankie and I traveled from our home, near Tahlequah, to Sequoyah's cabin, near Sallisaw. We collected seven things to take as gifts to Sequoyah. My words at the cave, as nearly as I can remember, were as follows:

"Osiyo Sequoyah (Oh-see-yoe See-gwoh-yah: Greetings Sequoyah). Nvwatoheyada ayv ehena (Nuhw-toe-hee-yah-dah ah-yuh aye-hay-nah: We come here in peace). I, Tsquayi, and my wife, Ajila (Ah-jee-lah; Fire), began our journey here from where you began your final journey, at your home in the Cherokee Nation. We bring you gifts and the regards of the Cherokee people.

"From your spring from which you drank, we bring ama (ah-mah; water), so you will not be thirsty. We bring gada (gah-dah; soil), from your field so that you will not miss your home. We bring hawiya (hah-wee-yah; meat), so that you will not be hungry. We bring selu isa (say-loo ee-sah; corn meal), so that you will not be hungry. We bring ama (ah-mah; salt), from your salt spring that was given to honor you by the Cherokee people. We bring jola (joe-lah; tobacco), for your pipe. We bring ajina (ah-jee-nah; cedar), the sacred tree of our people that grows in front of your cabin.

"Nvwatohiyada idehesdi. (Nuhw-toe-hee-yah-dah ee-day-hay-sdee: Let us live together in peace.)"

Conclusions

I believe that the spiritual evidence is very strong that the site we visited is the tomb of Sequoyah. Beside the three signs that we saw, I, and several others in the expedition, felt that they could sense the presence of Sequoyah in the cave and/or on the ranch. The vision of Charles by Gloria Rodriguez and the prophesy that a child would find the grave were both keys that opened the secret that had been kept locked for more than 150 years.

The scientific proof is not as strong and probably will never be conclusive. Conclusive proof would require exhuming the remains, and, by forensic or genetic testing or from articles buried with the body, proving that the remains were those of Sequoyah. That cannot be done without violating the grave and none on the expedition want that to happen.

There is, of course, considerable historical evidence to support the claim that this is the tomb of Sequoyah. The historical records showing that Cherokees lived in the area, that Sequoyah traveled to Mexico to convince those Cherokees to return to the Cherokee Nation, the Rodriguez family story that Sequoyah died and was buried in the cave, which is the only cave in the area, and the other family stories of the Rodriguez family are all evidence that the cave we visited is Sequoyah's tomb.

I believe there is meaning in the three signs that I saw. The white bear was the sign that I was supposed to witness the events that transpired. The redbird was the sign that the things we saw and heard were true. The rattlesnake was a warning; those who come to Sequoyah's tomb with a pure heart will be allowed to pass, but those who come to dishonor Sequoyah will suffer the wrath of the Eternal One.

Nvwatohiyada idehesdi. (Nuhw-toe-hee-yah-dah ee-day-hay-sdee; Let us live together in peace.)

Signed: Tsquayi, Udanvdi Ugvwiyuhi (Oo-dah-nuh-dee Oo-guh-wee-you-hee: Peace Chief) of the Cherokee Nation of Mexico

CHAPTER 38
BIRTH OF A NATION

In the last Chapter, I wrote about the discovery of the tomb of Sequoyah in early 2001. Later that year, under the leadership of President Fox of Mexico, the Constitution of Mexico was amended to recognize the indigenous peoples of Mexico, and guarantee them the right to their own nations with their own identity, language, property, schools, etc. The first group to be recognized under those new rights would be the Cherokees of Mexico. Frankie, and I were privileged to be invited to Mexico for that joyful and historic event.

To Mexico!

At noon on Tuesday, August 28, 2001, Frankie and I had just walked into our house in the Cherokee Nation after spending a month in Alaska. We were talking about the Cherokee National Holiday which would begin in three days, on Friday, August 31. The Cherokee Holiday is the biggest event of the year in the Cherokee Nation, during which we celebrate our heritage and the many thousands of visitors provide a tremendous boost for the local economy. It is the biggest weekend of the year for many businesses such as the B&B Frankie and I own and operate.

As I said, we had just walked into our house. Then, the phone rang. It was Dr. Charles Rogers of Brownsville, Texas with news of the impending recognition of the Cherokee Nation of Mexico! He wanted us to accompany him to the ceremony in Saltillo, the Capitol of the State of Coahuila on Friday, August 31. If we decided to go, we would have to leave the next day, Wednesday, and miss the Cherokee Holiday. Frankie and I spent ten minutes talking it over, but, in the end, we felt we could not miss that historic event. It was a once in a lifetime opportunity. Dr. Rogers started making our travel arrangements, while Frankie and I began throwing Alaska clothes out of our duffel bags and packing clothing for Mexico.

On Wednesday morning, we checked our mail and I had received a small box from a Cherokee friend in Idaho named Bob. It contained a letter and a gift. The letter so moved me that I took it on our trip, shared it with several people on the trip, and read an excerpt from it at the Council meeting I will tell you about later. I have included the letter at the end of this chapter.

On Wednesday afternoon, we flew to San Antonio where we joined Dr. Rogers and his family. On Thursday, we left on a chartered bus with about fifty others, most of them Texas Cherokees led by Chief Hicks. We traveled to Eagle Pass, Texas where Epigmenio and Gloria Rodriguez, Mexican Cherokees, and Al Kinsall, a local historian and newspaper writer, joined us. We crossed the border at Eagle Pass and continued across the Mexican desert to Saltillo. The trip from San Antonio to Saltillo took about eleven hours, during which Frankie and I became well acquainted with the our Texas Cherokee brothers and sisters. There was much joy on that bus.

The Ceremony

On Friday morning, we all dressed in Cherokee regalia, many of the men in turbans, ribbon shirts and moccasins and the women in shawls, head scarves and moccasins. A few of the men carried bows and arrows and I carried my cedar medicine staff. Our bus took us from our hotel through the narrow streets of Saltillo. We had a large banner on the bus, written in Spanish, telling of the occasion we were attending. All along the way, the people on the crowded sidewalks smiled and waved to us. We arrived at the State Palace of Coahuila and were immediately surrounded by a throng of reporters and TV cameras.

The ceremony took place in a great hall in the State Palace. The Mexicans are masters of pomp and ceremony. We were all seated around a great, rectangular table with a glass of water on a white napkin sitting before each place. We all rose when Governor Martinez y Martinez entered the room and took our seats when he seated himself at the head of the great table.

Introductions were made, and then, Chief Hicks smoked the Peace Pipe with the Governor. Next, one of the Governor's assistants proceeded to read, in Spanish, a rather lengthy account of the history of the Cherokees in the United States and in Mexico. Then, the Governor made some comments and then read the proclamation recognizing the Cherokee Nation of Mexico. Dr. Charles Rogers was designated as Principal Chief.

Then, the Governor presented several gifts to the new nation, including an eagle statue and a beautiful tapestry. Next, gifts were presented to the governor for the people of Coahuila State from the

Cherokee people. The largest gift was a check for ten million Mexican dollars, donated by Dr. Rogers, for the children of Coahuila. Frankie and I had brought soil from the Cherokee Nation in Oklahoma to be joined with the soil in the new Cherokee Nation in Mexico. I placed a small amount of soil in the hands of Dr. Rogers and the Governor who then joined them in a symbolic handshake. I also brought a hawk feather which I presented to the Governor with the words, "This is the feather of Tawodi, Hawk, Adanto Jisgwa, Spirit Bird of the Cherokees. I bring you the Spirit of the Cherokee People."

The First Council Meeting

That evening, in a conference room in our hotel, the first meeting of the Council of the Cherokee Nation of Mexico was held. Principal Chief Rogers named Chief D.L. Hicks as Red or War Chief, to be held for the remainder of his life, and asked me to serve as White or Peace Chief, likewise a lifetime appointment. I was also named Spiritual Counselor for the Cherokee Nation of Mexico.

The first order of business for the new Council was the nomination of three deceased and two living Cherokee women to be honored as "Beloved Woman" of the Cherokee Nation of Mexico. The deceased nominees were Chief Rogers' grandmother, Mary Price, Frankie's grandmother, Joanna Parris, and Chief Hicks' grandmother, Lucy Belle Hitt Hicks. The living nominees were Barbara Jean Layton Garrett and Mary Layton. All the nominees were approved by the entire Council.

The Cherokees of Mexico now have official recognition as Cherokees from a National and a State Government. It is my hope that, someday, all Cherokees in the United States will be recognized by the Government of the United States and by the

Cherokee Nation. Then, I would hope the next step would be the unification of all Cherokees into one nation, a half million strong. In today's world, there is power in numbers of votes. Through political power and cooperation among all Cherokees, we would have the chance to realize our full potential and our destiny.

Bob's Letter

As I said before, I received this letter on the day we left for our trip to Mexico, and it touched me. I have included the entire letter here.

Greetings friend.

It is a rare thing for me to write, I learned a long time ago that what I had to say did not mean much to people. My ignorance, I guess. These days my hand shakes so bad that even I can't read it anyway.

Your article, "Anikilohi", far more than made my day, it made my whole life. I know that it did also for many others, far more numbers than you will ever know. Don't worry about how many, just believe it.

Your words were exceptionally well chosen, they have strength, courage, power and the simplicity of the Truth. In my heart, I know that the spirit of the early ones who ran to the mountains and hid, are speaking to you. I do want you to understand, I know nothing of the "Way", such things were not allowed to be spoken of when I was a child beginning 63 years ago. I know nothing of what the tribe in Tahlequah has, does, nor anything other than what I read in your newsletter.

Yours and my friend, Todd, talk much. If one will take the time to stop, listen and look around, he can see that the knowledge of the ancient ones is returning, step by step, just like teaching a child, because that's what we are. Not this magical being that the white world teaches us that we are. We haven't risen above ignorance, we have degraded far below it to stupidity. That way we make better slaves to their system. Teach a child that Red is black and it will be black all his life.

In your words of power you said, "We need a Peace Chief....." How great that would be. But look at our world, someone always selects the Chief, gives him a badge of honour and it's done. The badge of honour does not a Chief make. He is created by the Creator, he is not made by hands. The Creator does this to one who listens to the spirit in his heart, simply by giving him knowledge and words of courage, power and the simplicity of the truth. His Honour is that of the Creator. Sadly, he is one most often not appreciated by the people, but those who seek knowledge love him dearly. Most often, it takes many years for the person who has the words of courage and power to realize who and what he actually is. My heart tells me that you have received a badge of Honour made without hands.

There is no doubt your clan is highly an honourable one, it would be an honour to be a small part of it. Whatever you do, be appreciative of it and protect it. As far as being an enrolled member of the tribe, it does not bother me that I cannot be. I am of the people who ran, fought and hid, they were brave hearts and I love them more every time I learn a small piece of new knowledge. I do thank them. I see people who ask, "My great, great, great grandmother was 1/16 Cherokee, if I get on the rolls, How much money will I get?" Knowledge? ZIP! In a way it is hurtful because the people of the tribe are saying to me, No, because you are not as good as we, and, in a way, maybe they are right, at least I look up to them.

The thing that has been a big bother to me since a small child, though it may sound ridiculous to you, is the simple fact that I am 63 years old and I still don't have a name. Ain't that a kick?

I wish I knew a way that your words could reach all of the wayward children. I do feel assured that your words will live and be read for a very, very long time to come. Keep listening to the Spirit and we shall learn from it, and destroy a little less.

I am enclosing a small gift so you will know that I speak from my heart. It was a gift from some Red Tailed friends who have lived near our home since spring. Many times they have done courtship maneuvers over our house with my wife Donna and I standing in our yard watching.

Gee-nah-lee-ee (Your Friend),
Bob

P.S. As far as being recognized by the Federallies, I would much rather be recognized by Elmer Fudd.

The Gift and the Name

The gift that Bob sent with his letter was the hawk feather that I presented to the Governor of Coahuila as the Spirit of the Cherokees. I have since given Bob the name Adanvto Tawodi (Ah-dun-toe Tah-woe-dee; Spirit Hawk).

193

CHAPTER 39
SAM HOUSTON

Sam Houston had a great effect on the history of America, and particularly the state of Texas. He also played an important role in the history of the Cherokee Nation. He was loved by the Cherokee people who called him Golanv (Goe-lah-nuh: The Raven), an old war title among the Cherokees.

Houston's Cherokee connections began early in his life. He was born in Virginia in 1793, but soon after his father's death when Sam was nine years old, his mother moved with him to Tennessee. Their home was on one side of the Tennessee River, and the territory of the Cherokees was on the other side. He worked on their farm and attended school, but he had an adventurous spirit. At age 16, he left home, crossed the river, and joined the Cherokees. He soon became a great favorite, and was adopted into the family of Chief Jolly. He lived with them for three years, during which time he wore Cherokee clothing, and learned the language and the ways of the Cherokees.

He then returned to the white man's world and enlisted as a private soldier under Andrew Jackson in the Creek War. He distinguished himself at the battle of Horseshoe Bend when he scaled the breastworks with an arrow in his thigh, and led his men into the thick of the enemy. His bravery won him the lasting admiration and friendship of Jackson.

He studied law and entered politics. He served two terms in Congress, and was elected Governor of Tennessee. He married a young lady, but two months later, without a word of explanation to any outsider, he left her, resigned as Governor and left Tennessee forever to join his old friends, the Cherokees, who had been forcibly removed from their homeland to Indian Territory. He settled near the home of his adopted father, Chief Jolly, who was now Principal Chief of the Cherokees. Later, Houston's wife in Tennessee divorced him and he married a beautiful Cherokee girl named Talihina who was the niece of Chief Jolly, and whom he had known when he was a boy living among the Cherokees.

In 1832, he visited Washington to plead the case of the Cherokees, wearing Cherokee clothing when he called upon President Jackson, who welcomed him as an old friend. Houston pleaded for the Cherokees to remain in their homeland, but unfortunately, President Jackson did not share Sam Houston's friendship for the Cherokees.

Soon afterward, Houston moved to Texas to take part in the effort to free Texas from Mexican rule. In 1836, Houston was a member of the convention that declared independence for Texas and in April of the same year, at the battle of San Jacinto he led 750 Texans who defeated Santa Ana's army of 1800. Houston's men inflicted upon the Mexicans the terrible loss of 630 killed and 730 taken prisoner, including

Santa Ana himself. Houston was badly wounded in the battle.

In the fall of 1836, he was overwhelmingly elected the first President of the Republic of Texas, and held the office for two years, and then retired. He was elected to the Texas Congress where he served until 1841, when he was again elected President of Texas. After Texas was annexed by the United States, Houston became a Congressman from Texas. From 1852 to 1860, his name was presented three times for nomination for President of the United States.

During his lifetime, often in the face of great criticism, Sam Houston remained the friend and staunch supporter of the Cherokees. While in the Texas Legislature, he attempted to allocate lands for the Texas Cherokees, but his efforts were defeated. He frequently declared that no treaty made and carried out in good faith had ever been violated by the Indians, but no treaty had ever been kept by the white people. His memory will always hold a place of honor in the hearts of the Cherokee people.

CHAPTER 40
HUCKLEBERRIES

I enjoy eating almost any food, but my favorite is huckleberries eaten directly from the bush. It may be coincidence that my beloved mentor, Kawaya, means Huckleberries in the Cherokee language. It may also be coincidence that, as a boy, my favorite book was Huckleberry Finn and Its author, Mark Twain is one of my favorite people and had a major influence on my writing. It may also be coincidence that a favorite former student of mine now studies huckleberries and their propagation, although, I don't recall ever mentioning my fondness for huckleberries while teaching. However, I don't think these facts are mere coincidence. There are things of the spirit that we learn or teach without intention or effort because they are part of our being. We could not prevent learning them or teaching them, even if we tried. Huckleberries are part of my being.

My former student tells me that there are

several species of huckleberries, and that they grow over much of North America, including Alaska. My experience with huckleberries is limited to those that grow on the high ridges of the Cherokee Nation in Northeastern Oklahoma. The bushes grow about two feet high, and the ripe berries are about the size of a garden pea, and dark blue to almost black in color.

Kawaya and I would roam the hills of the Cherokee Nation during June and July picking huckleberries. It took considerable time to fill the gallon lard pail because we ate as many as went into the pail. But eventually, we would bring a pail full home to my mother who would make them into huckleberry pies and other delights. She was a champion pie baker. Kawaya had a fondness for huckleberry pie, and he always took one home after a visit to our house during huckleberry season.

Another favorite huckleberry treat, of our family, was huckleberries and biscuits for breakfast. My mother would cook the huckleberries down until they floated in a syrup. We would break open biscuits and butter them, then spoon the huckleberries over them on our plate.

But, as I mentioned before, my favorite way to eat huckleberries was directly from the bush. The skins of ripe huckleberries, on the bush, have a coating; a pale, wonderful efflorescence, like nature congealed, which is destroyed by handling or washing the berries. Even picking them with the fingers disturbs this coating so I would often pick them with my mouth, grazing like a bear.

I remember one time, while picking, I ate a large amount of huckleberries, probably a gallon, and I started getting sick on the walk home. Then, I got very sick and threw up. My father didn't make me feel any better when he said I probably ate a spider! My mother said I probably wouldn't like huckleberries after getting sick on them, but the next day I was eating them again with as much pleasure as ever.

The number of huckleberries in the Cherokee Nation has decreased since I was a boy. Some of the old timers say it is because the woods don't burn off every year as was the custom in the old days. The Forestry Service puts the wildfires out before they burn far. My friend, Win Staples, who is a Wildlife Biologist in Alaska, says that the suppression of wild fires by the Forestry Service in Alaska has had a detrimental effect on the growth of native berries, and, subsequently, on the bears and other animals that feed on them. Hundred of years ago, Native Americans burned off areas to improve them for the growth of desirable plants, and to increase wildlife populations. Perhaps the Native Americans were not as ignorant as the white man thought.

These days, I get one or two messes of huckleberries a year, which is not enough for robust living, but will sustain life. Nowadays, there are many funds and organizations devoted to saving things like wetlands, endangered species of animals, etc. I wish someone would make an effort to save the huckleberry. Of course, the truth may be that I single-handedly ate them almost to extinction, and if I will just restrain myself for a few years, they will come back on their own.

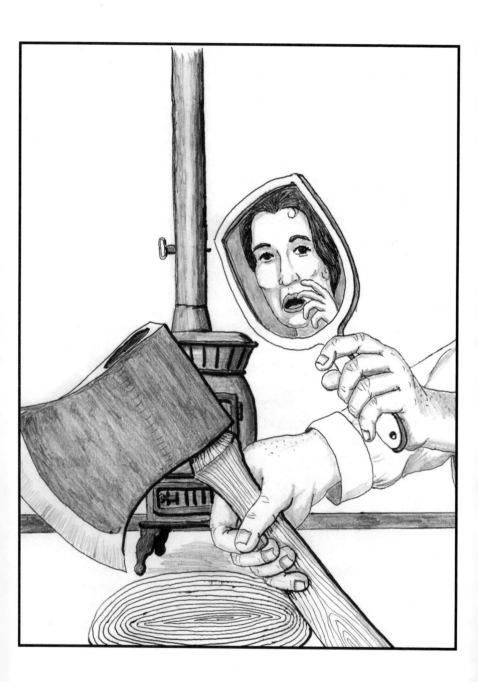

CHAPTER 41
CHOPPING WOOD

In our house, we have a fireplace, a wood burning stove for heating, and a wood burning cookstove. Over the years, I have cut most of the wood for these myself because I enjoy cutting wood. We have an abundance of good oak wood in the Cherokee Nation, which I consider the best wood of all for heating and cooking. Oak will produce almost as much heat as hickory and doesn't pop like hickory.

It is a joyful experience to be in the woods on a crisp fall or winter day, sawing a tree into lengths and then splitting them with an ax or maul. The sound of the wood splitting, and the smell of the fresh-cut oak are the things memories are made from.

I am competent with a chain saw and fully appreciate it because I used to cut wood with a crosscut saw. But I'm still not very good with an ax and that still bothers me, even though I have learned to live with it.

When I was a boy growing up in the Cherokee Nation, I admired the men in each community who were skilled with an ax. Their every movement with an ax was a picture of easy efficiency, more like a master musician with an instrument than a man with an ax. When cutting through a tree or log, every swing of the ax took out great chips of wood, and I was always surprised at how quickly the log was cut through. It seemed like they could chop for hours without tiring or losing any proficiency. When cutting a long stick up into shorter lengths, the stick was steadied over a larger stick or log with one foot, and the ax cuts were made dangerously close to the foot with complete confidence.

My own efforts with an ax were pitiful by comparison. My father told me I chopped like lightening--I never hit the same place twice. I did a few chores every evening for an elderly widow who lived down the road from our house. She was over eighty years old and walked with a crutch, but she could chop wood better than I.

Once, I asked her how she learned to chop wood. She chuckled and said that, the first Christmas after she was married, her husband gave her an ax and a mirror. He told her she could either learn to chop wood or sit and watch herself freeze to death!

I was determined that I would learn to use an ax with skill. Although I once stuck an ax in my knee, made gashes in several pairs of boots, almost killed my dog twice, and left scars on most of the trees on our place, I kept trying. Then, the discovery of girls and later college interrupted my pursuit of axcellence[17]. Years later, when I did get back to cutting wood, chain saws had made skill with an ax unnecessary. So, I never did learn to use an ax well.

To be completely honest and fair, however, I can't blame my failure totally on girls and chain saws. Lack of talent played a large part. We recognize that talent is required to play a musical instrument well, but overlook the fact that talent is also required to use an ax well. Each of us has things which we do easily which are difficult for others. Let us do those things, and be happy.

---

[17] If you like puns, this word is for you; if not, pretend it is a typographical error.

CHAPTER 42
THE FIREPLACE

I grew up around fireplaces, as did my father, grandfather and all my ancestors traced back to the cave. I can best express my feelings about fireplaces by saying I refuse to live in a house without one.

Of course, our fireplace is dirty, smelly, expensive and a lot of trouble, but so were our children, and we wouldn't have wanted to live without them either. An expert from the power company once came to do an energy audit on our house. He said bad things about my fireplace, after which, I threw him out of the house and sicced the dogs on him. But seriously, we have never questioned how much our fireplace is costing us; the joy it brings is beyond price. Having a fireplace is like buying a yacht, if you need to ask how much it costs, you can't afford it.

During the late fall, winter and early spring the fireplace is the center of activity in our home. On cool days, the fireplace provides all the heat we need, and on cold days, we supplement the fireplace with our wood-burning stove. There is always a fire in the fireplace because it provides a pleasant stimulation for the senses and brings a general feeling of contentment to our home.

I can tell if a home is heated by wood the moment I walk into it. Heat from a woodstove or fireplace feels different from gas or electric heat. Woodstoves are wonderful, but for me, they can't take the place of an open fireplace. The feel, the sight, the smell and the sound of an open fire stirs primal, forgotten feelings of security and contentment from deep within a person, which is not surprising when we consider that early humans probably spent one or two million years around open fires before the invention of stoves.

My idea of a fireplace is a campfire brought indoors, so I want it as uncontained and natural as possible. We have no glass doors or permanent screen on the front of our fireplace; we burn oak wood, which burns without popping, so that hot coals popping out on the floor are not a problem. We have a screen that we set up in front of the fireplace when we leave the house for an extended period of time.

We also don't use a grate in our fireplace, but have metal andirons to support the logs on each end. I let the ashes accumulate to the top of the cross members of the andirons, four or five inches deep, because I use the ashes to control the flow of air under the logs and thus control the rate at which the fire burns. I also use the ashes to "bank" the fire at bedtime, burying the hot coals. Next morning, I uncover the still glowing coals and use them to start a fire in a short time.

Through the cool and cold months, Frankie and I do a lot of our cooking in the fireplace. We have a swinging metal arm on which we hang black iron pots for boiling things like stew, chili, and beans. We use a Dutch Oven directly in the coals for roasting and baking. We also have a reflector oven we can set in front of the fire for baking. And of course, our kids and grandkids have roasted many wieners and marshmallows on green sticks or straightened coat hangers over the years.

In the last few years, since I have gotten serious about learning flint knapping, I have used our fireplace for heat-treating flint. I have a large skillet which I fill about half full of pea-sized gravel. I wrap the spalls of flint in aluminum foil and arrange them on top of the gravel. Then I fill the skillet level full with additional gravel and bury the skillet in the ashes with the top of the gravel exposed. Then I build a fire in the fireplace as usual and keep it burning all day until bed time. I let the skillet stay in the ashes with no fire burning until the following afternoon when it cools enough to remove. If it is removed from the ashes before that, the flint cools too quickly and will often fracture.

I'm not sure what temperatures I am reaching by this method but the treatment improves the chipping qualities of the local flint and some of it changes colors. I have used this same method, with the skillet, to heat-treat flint with an open fire outdoors with similar results. The prehistoric Native Americans used this method, without the skillet of course, to heat-treat flint, burying the flint spalls in sand or small gravel beneath their camp fires.

CHAPTER 43
A CHRISTMAS MIRACLE

Ginger was a small brown dog that was a member of our family and grew up with our children. She was about 17 years old when she left us on that snowy Christmas Eve, many years ago. But, I am getting ahead of my story.

Like most of the dogs we have had, Ginger came to us by accident. I had killed a bear with my bow on the White Mountain Apache Reservation in Arizona, and I had contacted a taxidermist in Tulsa about making the hide into a rug. Frankie and our son, Jay, went with me to Tulsa and searched for the taxidermist's house. We saw a lady working in her yard and pulled into her driveway to ask if she knew him. She knew him and directed us to his house. Then, she asked if we might want a little stray dog she had rescued from the street. We fell in love with the little dog and took her home with us.

Over the years, several other dogs, like "Chooch" and "Ring" and "Sam" and "Thumper" came and were part of our lives for awhile and then went away, but Ginger was always with us. She lived in our house, and played with our children in and around the river. She was with us as we traveled and camped across America, hunted squirrels and rabbits, shared countless adventures, and contributed in countless ways to our lives. Even when she grew old, in dog years, and our children had grown up and left home, she still remained feisty and loved to play. She would accompany me on my daily walks, run ahead and "hide" until I approached, then jump up and charge me, in mock attack, and then run ahead to set another ambush.

One evening, she didn't come in when I called her. I began searching and found her in our yard next to the river. She had evidently fallen from our catwalk, a height of about 12 feet onto some rocks in our yard, and she could not move the back half of her body. The veterinarian said that she had a spinal injury, and he did not think she would ever be able to use her back legs again.

After a week or so, I made a sling to support the back part of her body and started taking her for walks. We became a team; she would use her front legs and I became her back legs. I even learned when to lower her to a squat to relieve herself. Being summer, the weather was warm and I started taking her along when I went for my daily swim in the river. I began to notice some movement in her back legs when she swam.

By fall, she had regained most of the use of her back legs and walked and ran almost normally. Frankie and I, our children and now our grandchildren, enjoyed her for a few more years. We didn't know how old she was, because we didn't know how old she was when she came to us, but she had been with us about 15 years and we knew she had to be more than 17 years old. We noticed her bumping into things when she walked, and I found that her eyes were growing cloudy and she was going blind. She still went with me on walks down to the river, but I had to watch that she didn't hurt herself.

December 24 was sunny, and I put Ginger in our yard to get some sun. Our yard was fenced and the gate fastened so I knew she couldn't get out of the yard, even if she could find the gate. She liked to lay in the brown leaves beside our wood pile where the sun could warm her and she was protected from the wind. I made sure she was settled and went back to my work.

A sudden winter storm blew in late in the afternoon. The temperature suddenly dropped and a blowing snow started. I went out to get Ginger and she was not laying by the woodpile where I expected to find her. I called and looked everywhere in the yard, but I couldn't find her. I kept returning to the brown leaves around the woodpile because she was so nearly the color of the leaves I thought, perhaps, I was overlooking her. But, she was gone.

Although I knew she could not have gotten out of the yard, even if she had her sight, I frantically began searching outside the yard in the increasing snow. Darkness came and I continued with a flashlight; even going completely across the old bridge by our house.

I came back into the yard, heartsick with the knowledge that she was lost and afraid somewhere in that blinding snowstorm and knowing that she would not survive the night. I walked back to the woodpile and was shining my flashlight in a final, futile look when I saw something move!

A small, brown bird hopped from the leaves up onto my chopping-block, cocked its head to the side and looked at me. It was Ginger! I don't know how I knew it, but I did. In my mind, she told me not to worry or feel sadness; she was all right. Then she flew away into the nearby honeysuckle vines.

I did not believe what had happened. I searched again the next day and for several more days, wanting at least to find her and give her a proper burial. I even searched down the river, in my boat, in case she had fallen into the river. Many years have passed now and I have never found a trace of her. I have gradually accepted the fact that a miracle did occur on that Christmas Eve, and that Ginger did turn into a little brown bird and fly away.

Now, when I go on my daily walks, sometimes a flock of little brown birds goes with me. They fly along the trail ahead of me and alight in the bushes or on the ground until I get within a few steps, and then they flare up, fly ahead and alight again, time after time, apparently enjoying their little game. I call them "Ginger's Children."

CHAPTER 44
EAGLES, WHITE BUTTERFLIES AND GRANDBABIES

In 1996, Frankie and I helped to welcome two new grandbabies, one in Alaska and one in Tahlequah. I want to tell you about some unusual things that happened before the birth of each. The Cherokees of olden times believed that such things were signs that foretold something about the gifts of the person the baby would become, or about something the person would accomplish during his or her life.

During the winter, before the new grandbabies were born, I saw an unusual number of Bald Eagles along the Illinois River by our house. The eagle has always been a sacred bird to the Cherokees, said to carry messages to the Spirit World. I have a special relationship with all birds. In a very real sense, the birds speak to me, and I speak to them. I have an especially close relationship with eagles. We cherish and honor one another.

The eagle's main diet is fish. Each winter when the water freezes over in Alaska, the eagles migrate south to the many lakes and streams of the Cherokee Nation where the water doesn't freeze over, and they can catch fish all winter. In late winter, they fly back to Alaska to nest and rear their young.

The eagles usually leave the Cherokee Nation in February, and I had never seen them along the river after the last of February. That spring, I saw some along the river during the first week of March. I thought to myself that it would be nice to see an eagle on my birthday, which is March 13. On March 13th, I saw three great eagles; two had white heads and the third was an immature with a dark head. Each greeted me with a special gesture or salute which eagles show to their siblings. During flight, they flip upside down for an instant and reach up with their talons like they are catching something above them. I told them I was honored to be considered their brother.

The three eagles remained along the river near our house through the month of March. During that time, Frankie and I decided we would travel to Alaska in June to be present for the birth of our daughter Jane's and her husband Todd's baby. On March 28, I gave the three eagles a message to take to Alaska, and evidently they left the next day because I did not see them along the river again.

On May 28, Frankie and I flew into Kenai, Alaska, which is about eighty miles from Homer, where Jane and Todd live, because we wanted to visit friends in Kenai. Jane and Todd left a car for us in Kenai to drive to Homer the next day. As we came over the crest of the ridge and began our descent down to Homer by Kachemak Bay, a great eagle was hovering directly over the highway, as if in welcome. On the road to Jane and Todd's house, we saw two more eagles, each directly over the road. I laughed

214

and told Frankie they were the eagles that had been on the river near our house and they were welcoming us to their home.

Many eagles flew around Jane and Todd's house every day. Their house sat high on the ridge above Homer and the eagles loved to ride the updrafts that come from the bay and up the slopes. Three pairs of eagles had built nests in the tall spruce trees below the house and each day during the three weeks we were there, we looked down into their nests with binoculars while they tended their eggs and then their young.

When Jane went into labor on June 7, we accompanied Todd and her to the hospital, and as we parked the car, a great eagle circled just above us, and then flew over the doorway of the hospital as if showing us the way.

Jane and Todd's new son, and Frankie and my new grandson, weighed ten pounds and eight ounces. They named him Luke Eagle Phillips.

That brings me to the beginning of the second part of this story. While at Jane and Todd's house in Alaska, I noticed that all the butterflies I saw in their yard, and in the surrounding forest were white. I remarked about it to Frankie because in the Cherokee Nation, white butterflies are rare.

Among the ancient Cherokees, the kamama (kah-mah-mah; butterfly) was said to show the medicine people which plants would cure sickness. Any white animal, bird, etc. was considered sacred, so the white butterfly was considered sacred. Legends tell that a white butterfly brought the Cherokee alphabet, which allowed the Cherokees to have a written language, to Sequoyah in a dream.

On June 20, the day after Frankie and I returned from Alaska to the Cherokee Nation, I saw a white butterfly near our house. I told Frankie about it, laughed, and said it must have gotten into our luggage in Alaska. The next day I saw another, in a location several miles away so I'm sure it wasn't the same one. Over the next two weeks, I saw a total of seven white butterflies. Frankie laughed and said I needed to see one more so there would be one for each of our seven grandchildren plus the one that was due to be born soon to our son, Jay, and his wife, Melissa, who lived in Tahlequah.

On July 8, 1 saw the eighth white butterfly. The next day, Jay and Melissa's first child, and Frankie and my new granddaughter and eighth grandchild was born. She weighed seven pounds and thirteen ounces. They named her Baylee Rae Herrin and Frankie and I gave her the Cherokee name, Kamama.

CHAPTER 45
MUD DAUBERS

I have always considered mud daubers to be my friends because I have never been stung by one, and I support anyone who tries to control the spider population. But, I feel that the mud daubers have taken advantage of our friendship and are becoming a nuisance. In fact, they are driving me crazy!

In case you don't know about mud daubers, they are the slim-waisted, solitary wasps that build tube nests of mud on the walls of barns, attics, etc. After completing a nest, the mud dauber hunts spiders, paralyzes them with a sting and stuffs them inside the nest. When the nest is full with dozens of spiders, the mud dauber lays an egg inside the nest, then seals the opening with mud. The egg hatches a worm inside which eats the spiders, develops into an adult mud dauber, eats through the wall of the nest and flies away to build its own nest and continue the cycle.

I don't kill mud daubers when I find them on the window screens trying to get out of our house. I don't know how they get into the house, but they do. I catch them in a handkerchief, folded several times to protect me from their stingers, carry them outside and release them. Earlier this summer. I would catch and release one every few days. The frequency increased until it was one every day. I joked to Frankie that I thought it was the same one each time returning because it knew I would carry it back outside.

The crisis that is driving me crazy developed this past week. One of our little granddaughters came to stay with us for a few days, and the first morning she came out of the upstairs bathroom with eyes as big as saucers. There were "waspers" in the bathroom! And she wasn't going back in there until Pap-Pap took care of them.

I found five mud daubers on the screen of the bathroom window and carried the first four, one at a time, down the stairs and out the front door. I was carrying the last mud dauber down the stairs and our granddaughter, who could wait no longer, darted into the bathroom without bothering to close the door behind her. As I neared the front door, the mud dauber escaped from my fingers. I didn't see which way it flew, but a moment later, I knew where it was when I heard our granddaughter scream and abdicate the throne.

Now, before our grandchildren will enter the bathroom, I have to clear out the mud daubers. I am wearing out my legs running up and down the stairs. I still consider the mud daubers to be my friends, but I will be glad when cold weather gets here so they will hibernate and I can get some rest.

CHAPTER 46
THE HORNET'S NEST

A few years ago, in November, I found a hornet's nest in the woods near our house. I was cutting some firewood for winter and happened to look up and see the nest. It was unusually large and beautiful; I guessed it to be two feet long and a foot in diameter and perfectly shaped. It was about 25 feet above the ground in an oak tree, and I immediately started thinking about how to get it. A large hornet's nest is a prize, if you are lucky enough to find one.

Of course, it is a good idea to make sure the hornets are finished with a nest before you get it. I have heard stories of people who found hornet's nests in the late fall or winter, and assuming the hornets were all gone, hung them inside their house. The dormant hornets inside the nest revived in the warm house and came out, creating a lively time for everyone!

I studied the nest carefully with my binoculars. Although the day was warm, I thought the weather had been cold long enough for the hornets to have abandoned the nest. But, I spied a few hornets zipping in and out of the nest and quickly decided I wanted no part of them. I have been stung by hornets and, each time, I thought I had been struck by lightening!

I returned to the nest after a cold spell in December, and seeing no hornet activity, climbed the tree to get the nest. It was even more beautiful up close; it was striped with dark and light bands of color where the hornets had used different kinds of wood to make the paper for constructing the nest. My eyes moved from the sides of the nest to the opening at the bottom, and I discovered three hornets looking back at me!

I suddenly remembered urgent business elsewhere. Someone watching me would have had trouble deciding whether I climbed or fell out of the tree, but it did not take me long to reach the ground. I determined that most of my injuries were probably not fatal and went home.

In January, after a big sleet storm, I figured it was time to get the nest. As I approached the tree, something gray lying on the sleet covered ground caught my eye. It was a piece of striped gray paper from a hornet's nest. Fearing the worst, I quickly moved to the tree and looked for the nest.

Only about half the nest remained, hanging in shreds, and the ground around the tree was strewn with the remains of the nest. A bird or squirrel, searching for dormant hornets or larvae, had torn the nest to pieces. I don't know which made me feel worse; not getting the nest or the thought that some bird or squirrel was braver than I.

CHAPTER 47
THE CHEROKEES IN INDIAN TERRITORY

I was digging on the river bank beside our house and found some old buried cables and a faded sign that said "Cherokee". A few days later, quite by chance, I was reading in the **Indian-Pioneer History Papers** of the Oklahoma Historical Society and I found reference to a ferry that crossed the Illinois River at this location. The papers also contained several interesting observations about Cherokee life in Indian Territory, now Oklahoma, in the period between the Trail of Tears in 1839 and Oklahoma statehood in 1907. I want to share some of those things with you. I will indicate, with quotation marks, which are direct quotes from the **Indian-Pioneer History Papers**.

From Vol. 10, page 483: "There was an old ferry established three and a half miles east of Tahlequah, Oklahoma, just a few yards south of where the 62 highway bridge crosses the Illinois River."

This is the exact location of our house, and the cables I found must have been for the ferry. In the woods behind our house, an old road is cut into the steep riverbank and was evidently used to get wagons, and later, cars down to the ferry.

The description of the ferry continues, "This ferry was first established by the Boudinots. Later, it was operated by Mart Miller of Tahlequah and then by Andrew McCarter of Tahlequah. It was abandoned when the bridge was erected across the river. Just before the bridge was finished, Mr. McCarter had a man hired to operate the ferry. One day, he started to set a man across the river in an old T Model Ford. As the man drove on board, the car had bad brakes, so he could not stop and he hit the ferryman, knocked him off the boat and drowned him."

The old bridge that replaced the ferry still stands near our house, although it has been closed for many years. The **Indian-Pioneer History Papers** list five ferries that crossed the Illinois River at various locations. The other four were at Gore, Cookson, Park Hill and Chewey. I think there was another ferry, operated by a family named Tenkiller, which is not on the list. The actual name for Tenkiller Lake on the Illinois River, is Tenkiller Ferry Reservoir. When the river level was low enough, people forded the river, and didn't have to pay the toll for the ferry.

A glimpse of life in those times is furnished by and interview with Wallace Thornton on page 491: "All the clothes we had were made from cotton and wool which we raised. We picked the seeds out of the cotton, washed it and spun it into thread and wove it into cloth with which to make our clothes. For many nights I have sat up and spun cotton and I worked especially hard if I was going to get a new shirt.

"We also tanned our own cow hides to make our shoes. We had no tacks so we had to use pegs made out of wood.

"We had different trades for different men to follow just as we have today. There were men who

222

did nothing but build spinning wheels and sell them. Others built looms. Some made cards to card the cotton and wool on, and some made shoes to sell. But all of these things were made by hand. There was no machinery--just a pocket knife, an ax, saw and plane. These, too, were made at home.

"We had no matches either. If it rained and put out our fire, we had to start another by striking a spark from a piece of flint into some gun powder and lint cotton.

"We had no ropes then and had to make our plow lines from the bark of Po-Po trees. In the spring when the sap would rise, we would find a tall Po-Po tree and peel the bark from the ground to the top. Then we would split this into narrow strips and plait four strands together, making a nice round rope."

From Volume 95, page 58 is an interview with E. F. Vann, who said: "Most of the people lived in log cabins of one or two rooms, some of which had only dirt floors while some were puncheon floors. In almost all these cabins there was a large stone or stick and mud fireplace. The wealthier mixed blood and full blood families lived in larger houses of frame, log, brick, or stone which were equal to homes back in the states during this period.

"The people lived a simple life and much of what they had to eat and wear was produced at home. They killed and cured their own beef, pork and venison. They dried their meat by placing it on scaffolds and under the scaffolds they would keep smoldering fires allowing the smoke to pass over and around the meat to keep away flies and insects while the sun did the drying. They ground their own corn in a mortar with a pestle or ram. They picked the seeds from cotton by hand. Cotton and wool were carded, spun and woven into cloth, and spinning wheels and hand looms were found in nearly every well-regulated home.

"People were hospitable and delighted to entertain friends and neighbors. Their social affairs and popular sports consisted of picnics, fishing parties, horse racing, ball plays, fox hunts and house raisings as well as Stomp dances and church going.

"In the Flint District and in surrounding districts, except in the clearings which were being tilled, the country was still in its original condition, a hill country of forest with small areas of prairie scattered through it. It seemed the entire country abounded with wild game, deer, bear, opossum, raccoon, wild hogs, wild cattle, wild horses, bob cats, squirrels, rabbits, wild turkeys, quail, prairie chicken and wild pigeons. Antelope and buffalo were on the great prairies to the west in what was called the Cherokee Strip and which could be reached from the Cherokee Nation by a three or four days journey. Many hunting parties were formed to go hunt buffalo in what the hill Cherokees called the buffalo country.

"The proverbial bow and arrow was the most used weapon in the early days but many owned cap and ball rifles which were used for killing large game like deer, bobcats and bear. Almost every little Indian boy had a blowgun with which he killed birds.

"I loved to hunt and fish. I would gig fish or shoot them with a bow and arrows and I killed birds with a blowgun made from cane and I killed large game with a cap and ball rifle. I bought gun caps and powder at the store, some bar lead and molded my own rifle balls.

"All species of soft water fish were abundant in the creeks and rivers and particularly in the Barren Fork and Illinois River.

"Wild bees were common and the Indians could have plenty of honey by cutting down a "bee tree" and robbing the bees of their treasure.

"Some orchards were planted, but not many because there were plenty of wild fruits and berries such as plums, grapes, seedling peaches, dewberries, huckleberries and a number of others.

"Each fall, many nuts were gathered such as pecans, walnuts, hazel nuts and chinquapins as well as hickory nuts."

Hickory nuts were usually made into kanvchi (kah-nuh-chee). Kanvchi is made by pounding the hickory nuts, shells and meats, until it has a dough-like consistency and can be formed into round balls about the size of a baseball. When Kanvchi is wanted to eat, the ball is placed in hot water which dissolves the nut meats from the shells. The liquid can be drunk or mixed with hominy or rice and eaten.

Mr. Vann then describes Cherokee life after the Civil War: "The end of the War found the Cherokees in a pitiable condition with their homes burned, fields grown up with weeds, live stock eaten or driven off and hogs and cattle wild in the cane brakes. It took about ten or twelve years after the end of the Civil War for the Cherokees to re-establish themselves and to recover from the effects and losses of the Civil War.

"Soon lands were taken from the Cherokees on which wild Indians were placed on reservations. From the close of the Civil War the Cherokees continued to lose their lands in first on way and then another until allotments were made by the Dawes Commission."

When I (Al Herrin) was a boy growing up in the Cherokee Nation in the 1940's and 50's, many of the things described in the **Indian-Pioneer History Papers** were still in common practice. Our family always butchered several hogs in the fall of the year, as soon as the weather turned cold. The butchering took place out of doors. My father would shoot the hog, then stick it in the throat with a knife to bleed it out. Cuts were then made in the hock joints of the hind legs, a short pole was inserted through the tendons, and the hog was hung up with block and tackle. A metal, 55 gallon barrel half full of water was heated on a fire, and the hog was dipped into the boiling water to loosen the hair, which was then scraped off the hide. When I was a small child, my job was to keep the fire well supplied with wood. Later, when I was old enough, I helped with the butchering.

My mother had a large kettle set up on another fire, nearby, in which she rendered out the fat to make lard or, mixed it with lye, to make soap. We had a smoke-house in which we cured and smoked the meat. My father was well known in the community for his excellent smoked hams, bacon and turkeys.

Today, Cherokees own only a small percentage of the land within the Cherokee Nation, which makes up a fourteen county area in Northeastern Oklahoma. Most of the land, and particularly the fertile river bottom land, is owned by non-Cherokees. The land still owned by Cherokees mainly lies on the rocky, infertile ridges of the hills.

CHAPTER 48
THE AMAZING CHEROKEES

I am proud to be Cherokee. The Cherokees are truly amazing. It has been estimated that, before the arrival of Columbus, there were about 350 distinct Native American tribes in what is now the United States. Of those, the Cherokees have accomplished several things that make them unique among all the tribes and nations.

Perhaps foremost among these accomplishments was the development of a written language. The story of Sequoyah and his twelve years of work to develop the written language is, in itself, amazing. The written language was amazing; it was so constructed that a Cherokee speaker could learn to read and write in a very short period of time, sometimes in only a few days. Within a few years of its introduction, almost every Cherokee could read and write. The literacy rate in the Cherokee Nation in the 1830's was probably higher than is the literacy rate in the United States today.

Those amazing accomplishments produced other amazing accomplishments. The Cherokees wrote down many of the details of their daily life, culture and religion, along with their sacred myths. Medicine men and women recorded the ingredients of their medicines, and the sacred rituals performed to heal the sick. In other tribes, small amounts of information of this type were recorded by European observers, but the Cherokees were the only Nation that recorded these things themselves, so the information is more complete and accurate than for any other tribe.

The Cherokees established a newspaper, The Phoenix, which they printed on their own printing press, in the Cherokee language. They printed books, including the Bible, and established a system of schools that were equal or superior to any schools of the white settlements that surrounded their territory. They established a system of government, patterned after the United States, with a Constitution, written laws, courts, etc. Those were the "savages" that were rounded up by federal troops and forcibly removed from their homeland to Indian Territory in 1839. Thousands died on the "Trail Where They Cried."

The next amazing accomplishment of the Cherokees was the recovery from the removal. The Cherokees have never been a people to dwell on the past; we look forward. The Cherokees rebuilt their nation, their schools, and their lives in Indian Territory to equal what they had lost in their homeland.

I could list other amazing accomplishments of the Cherokee people and individual Cherokees, but I believe I have presented enough evidence to support my contention that the Cherokees are amazing. But, there is one final amazing accomplishment of the Cherokees that I will mention because it has been very important to me, personally. I refer to the preservation of the art of making the traditional Cherokee bows and arrows.

I grew up shooting traditional Cherokee bows and arrows, and learned to make them myself. I learned from my Cherokee Elders who had learned from their Elders, and so on back through time.

One day in the 1980's, I found a book called **Native American Bows** by T. M. Hamilton, a respected archaeologist, and published by the Missouri Archaeological Society. I was amazed when I read Mr. Hamilton's observations concerning the bows and arrows of what is now the Eastern United States. He wrote, "Since this area was the first to be settled or, at least , invaded by the white trader, the bow, as a serious weapon, has long since disappeared; our museums today are almost entirely lacking in aboriginal, or near aboriginal, specimens. The haste with which the natives east of the Mississippi abandoned the bow in favor of the gun is in marked contrast to the way the Plains Indians continued to rely upon the bow into the third quarter of the 19th Century. From this we can conclude that either the bow of the Eastern woodlands was not so effective or the conditions of war and hunting were not so favorable to its use." In the next paragraph, he continues, "Therefore, it can safely be said that by 1700, every Indian from the Atlantic to the Mississippi had heard of the gun and was clamoring for one, and the art of making good bows went into rapid decline."

In fairness to Mr. Hamilton, the art of bowmaking was lost to all the Eastern tribes and eventually to all the tribes across the continent, with the exception of the amazing Cherokees. I realized that I was the recipient of an amazing and, heretofore, secret legacy and I decided it should be revealed to the world.

I wrote the book, **Cherokee Bows and Arrows**, began publishing the **White Bear Newsletter**, and writing articles about Cherokee bows and bowhunting for several newspapers and magazines. When I began, bowmaking was almost a lost art, even among the Cherokees, and the compound bow seemed destined to make traditional archery obsolete.

Today, many thousands of bowyers across the United States, around the world, and in the Cherokee Nation are making traditional Native American bows and arrows, and using them to shoot targets and to hunt. For my work in preserving the art of making traditional Cherokee bows and arrows, I have been designated a "Cherokee National Living Treasure" by the Cherokee Nation. I am proud to have played a small part in preserving the culture of the amazing Cherokees. I am proud to be Cherokee.

CHAPTER 49
CHIEF DROWNING BEAR

Chief Yonagvska (Yoe-nah-guh-skah; Bear drowning him/her) was recognized as Chief of the East or Keetoowah Cherokees living on the waters of the Oconaluftee and Tuckasegee in the Cherokee Homeland before the removal. He was a strikingly handsome man, standing six feet three inches tall, and strongly built. He was a Peace Chief and a great orator, and he succeeded in keeping some of his people in their Cherokee Homeland when the Cherokee Nation was removed to Indian Territory in what is now Oklahoma.

He was a prophet and reformer as well as a Chief. When he was about sixty years old, he had a severe illness which terminated into a coma. His family thought he was dead but, after twenty-four hours, he revived. He told them he had been to the Spirit World where he had talked to his family and friends who had passed over before, and he had talked to God. God had told him to return to life with a message for his people, and that he would call him home again at a later time.

Chief Yonagvska was recognized as the greatest orator of all the Chiefs of the Cherokees, and he brought all his talents and power to a fight against the evils of whiskey. He had been addicted to alcohol himself before his illness, but afterwards, he stopped drinking and organized his people into a temperance society. To do this, he called his people together into a council and then, in an eloquent speech that moved many in his audience to tears, he declared that God had sent him with the message that whiskey should be banished from among them. From that time, until after his death, whiskey was unknown among the East Cherokees.

The white Government brought frequent pressure upon Chief Yonagvska to remove his people to the West with the rest of the Cherokees. He resisted all attempts, however, stating that his people were safer from aggression among their rocks and mountains than they could ever be in a land which the white man could find profitable. He said the Cherokees could be happy only in the country where nature had planted them. Although he resisted efforts to remove his people from their homeland, he always counseled peace and friendship with the white man.

He always maintained his traditional Cherokee religion, and he was suspicious of the white missionaries. When the Bible was translated into the Cherokee language and the Sequoyah syllabary, a missionary brought a copy of the Book of Matthew for the people to read. But Chief Yonagvska would not allow his people to read it until he read it himself. After reading it, the old Chief dryly remarked, "Well, it seems to be a good book--strange that the white people are not better, after having had it so long."

Chief Yonagvska died, some said from a broken heart, at age eighty, in April of 1839, a few months after the removal of the Cherokee Nation over the "Trail Where They Cried."

CHAPTER 50
THE CHEROKEE NATION TODAY

Many first-time visitors to the Cherokee Nation of Oklahoma expect to find the Cherokees living on a reservation, in tipis, and wearing deerskin clothing and feathered headdresses. Actually, there is no reservation, and Cherokees live in the same kind of houses, and wear the same kinds of clothing as do most citizens of the United States. I will familiarize you with some facts about the Cherokee Nation and the Cherokees so that you will know what to expect if you come to visit.

We Cherokees have the unique status of being citizens of two nations, the Cherokee Nation and the United States of America, as well as citizens of the state of Oklahoma. The government of the United States recognizes the Cherokee Nation, and all other Nations and Tribes of Native Americans, as self-governing nations within the boundaries of the United States. The state of Oklahoma also recognizes the right of self-government by the Cherokees and other Nations and Tribes in Oklahoma.

The government of the Cherokee Nation is based on a Constitution that provides for Executive, Legislative and Judicial branches. The Chief and members of the Tribal Council are elected by the people and the Judges are appointed for life terms.

The Capitol of the Cherokee Nation of Oklahoma is Tahlequah, a modern town of about thirteen thousand. The Cherokee Nation includes fourteen counties of Northeastern Oklahoma. The number of persons enrolled as members of the Cherokee Nation is about 240,000, although, many of those are residents of other states. The Cherokee Nation is the second largest tribe of Native Americans, after the Navaho. The Cherokees in North Carolina are a separate entity, known as the Eastern Cherokees. They have a reservation at Cherokee, North Carolina. Another group of Cherokees recognized by the U.S. Government is the Keetoowah Band with headquarters at Tahlequah.

I mentioned that, in Oklahoma, we Cherokees do not have a reservation. Back in the late 1800's, some clever U.S. Government bureaucrat figured out a way to steal more Cherokee land. The U.S. Government had ceded large tracts of land in Indian Territory to the Cherokee Nation in exchange for land taken from the Cherokees in our homeland in the East. But, then came the clever idea; instead of letting the Cherokee Nation collectively own all the land ceded, individual Cherokees would each be allotted a parcel of land, leaving a huge amount of land left over that the U.S. Government could then open for non-Cherokee settlement.

During the time since the allotments, the allotted parcels of Cherokee land have been divided among descendents, sold or lost for taxes until many Cherokees own little or no land. Most of the land within the boundaries of the Cherokee Nation is owned by non-Cherokees. Despite the efforts of the

Cherokee Nation to assist with better housing, industries to provide jobs, health and education services and programs to promote pride in the Cherokee culture, many Cherokees live in poverty, physically and psychologically obscured by the dominant white culture.

As a result, many Cherokees have low self-esteem, and low expectations for themselves and their children. The rates of school drop-outs, teen pregnancy, alcohol and drug abuse, physical and mental health problems, suicide, and about any other undesirable condition you can imagine, are higher among the Cherokees than among the dominant white population. That is, of course, no different than for most of the nations and tribes of Native Americans throughout the Americas.

In spite of our problems, I do not want to live anywhere else. The Cherokee people still maintain a friendly, caring spirit and a sense of humor beyond any people I have ever known. Visitors come to the Cherokee Nation by the tens of thousands to enjoy our beautiful, clear streams and lakes, our hills and forests, and our truly friendly people. We are survivors, strong because we have been tested. As a people, we are searching for our unique identity, and a position of honor in the world. I believe we will find both, and hopefully, sooner rather than later.

CHAPTER 51
THE CHEROKEE PURPOSE

Many years ago, the revered Cherokee religious leader, Redbird Smith, said, "I have always believed that the Great Creator had a great design for my people, the Cherokees. I have been taught that, from my childhood up, and now, in my mature manhood, I recognize it as a great truth. Our forces have been dissipated by the external forces; perhaps it has been just a training, but we must now get together as a race and render our contribution to mankind. We are endowed with intelligence, we are industrious, we are loyal and we are spiritual, but, we are overlooking the particular Cherokee mission on earth, for no man nor race is endowed with these qualifications without a designed purpose."

I believe, as Redbird Smith, that we have a great purpose and that the first step of the Cherokees toward rendering our contribution to mankind must be to "get together", and establish peace and unity among all Cherokees. It is toward that goal that I have worked for many years. The establishment of the Cherokee Nation of Mexico, and its recognition by the Government of Mexico is an important step toward the recognition of all Cherokees, and our unification into one great nation. Then, perhaps we can join with all Native Americans in a great alliance. That was the dream of our Shawnee brother, Tecumseh. If we will work together as brothers and sisters, we can magnify the power of God.

But those are only the first steps. I believe the mission of the Cherokees is to show the world the path to peace. We will do this by teaching the true spiritual relationships among persons, Nature, and the Spirit World. Whether we use the name God, Yahweh, Allah, Eternal One, Great Spirit, or some other, we call upon the same being. I have never seen proof that any nation, religious sect, race, sex, or even species, is favored by God over any other. We must humble ourselves, rise above intolerance of others, and in our hearts, replace hate and indifference with acceptance and respect. I believe, with all my being, that we will accomplish that mission.

CHAPTER 52
THE FRUIT OF THE SPIRITS

In the Judeo-Christian Bible, the Apostle Paul listed the "Fruit of the Spirit" in Galatians, Chapter 5, as love, joy, peace, long-suffering, gentleness, goodness, faith, meekness and temperance and states that "against such there is no law".

I say that God does not condemn any Cherokee who, with a pure heart, seeks the seven fruits of the Cherokee spirits: truth, goodness, beauty, love, enlightenment, fulfillment, and peace. The seekers of those fruits are the people that the ancient Cherokees called "Aniyvwiya" (Ah-nee-yuh-wee-yah; Human Beings). I tell you that God and Nature protect and nurture the Aniyvwiya. I tell you further that there are people with pure hearts, seekers of the fruits of the spirits, found in every race and every creed throughout the world. I call them all Aniyvwiya, my brothers and sisters, and tell them that God will protect and nurture them. My brother, Black Elk, of the Ogallala Sioux said, "The power of a pure and good soul is planted as a seed, and will grow in man's heart as he walks in a holy manner. The Spirit is anxious to aid all who seek him with a pure heart".

But, beware the wrath of God. I say to you that God does condemn those persons, found in every race and every creed, that twist the word of God to serve their own selfish goals. Those persons lead lives that are out of balance, and the spirits and Nature do not know them.

Their institutions of worship have failed to bring the promised "peace on earth and good will toward men" because they preach that their narrow, twisted "truth" is the only truth, and that God has chosen them above others. They seek blessings for their members rather than for all mankind. They have caused division between nations and creeds rather than promoting tolerance and brotherhood. They have promoted blind ignorance and opposed the search for knowledge. They have promoted the subjugation of women, Nature and any people different from themselves rather than honoring all life and all spirit. As a result of those actions, the fruit they have produced has been "wars and rumors of war", rather then peace on earth. I offer the history of the world for the past five-thousand years as proof of the truth of my words.

I say that the time of the Aniyvwiya has come. Let the Aniyvwiya in every nation, race and creed speak out, and let each one believe that his or her words can make a difference in the world. Let us believe that the people of the world will recognize our words of truth and follow. Let us believe that, through the power of God, peace on earth is possible.

Nvwtohiyada idehesdi (Nuhw-toe-hee-yah-dah ee-day-hay-sdee; Let us live together in peace).